GEOFF ROLLS

CLASSIC CASE STUDIES
IN PSYCHOLOGY

Hodder Arnold

A MEMBER OF THE HODDER HEADLINE GROUP

Dedication

To Eve, Billy and Ella

Orders: please contact Bookpoint Ltd; 130 Milton Park, Abingdon, Oxon OX14 4SB.
Telephone: 44 (0)1235 827720. Fax: 44 (0)1235 400454. Lines are open from 9.00–5.00,
Monday to Saturday, with a 24-hour message answering service. You can also order through our website
www.hoddereducation.co.uk

**If you have any comments to make about this, or any of our other titles, please send them to
educationenquiries@hodder.co.uk**

British Library Cataloguing in Publication Data
A catalogue record for this title is available from the British Library

ISBN-10: 0 340 88692 7
ISBN-13: 978 0 340 88692 2

This edition published 2005
Impression number 10 9 8 7 6 5 4 3
Year 2009 2008 2007 2006

Typeset by Phoenix Photosetting, Chatham, Kent.
Printed in India for Hodder Arnold, an imprint of Hodder Education, a member of the Hodder
Headline Group, 338 Euston Road, London NW1 3BH

Contents

Foreword

Open any textbook of psychology and you'll find a definition of the subject that refers to 'science'. Psychology is widely accepted as being 'the scientific study of mind and behaviour', and it has traditionally modeled itself on the natural sciences (physics and chemistry in particular). But there has always been heated debate as to the nature of science and the validity of trying to study the human mind and its outward expression (behaviour) using methods (in particular, the laboratory experiment) drawn from the natural sciences.

For those 'hard-nosed' scientific psychologists who believe that the experiment is the 'method of choice', case studies – the in-depth investigation of an individual, a pair of individuals (such as twins), or an entire family – lie at the opposite end of the scientific spectrum. Most case studies are based on one or two individuals (rather than groups of varying size), and are often derived from the work of *clinicians* (psychologists, psychiatrists and others who work with people experiencing psychological difficulties or mental disorders). In these cases, the psychologist or psychiatrist doesn't set out to test a theory with a view to publishing the results, as those conducting experiments do. The case study is a spin-off, a usually unexpected outcome of their work with particularly interesting and unusual – even unique – patients or clients. As the hard-nosed psychologist sees it, while such studies may be interesting in themselves, they are of little scientific value. Why? Because no other psychologist can repeat or replicate the study, which is a feature of experiments that makes them so attractive.

But doesn't this miss the point? Isn't it precisely the uniqueness and novelty of the individuals who become the subject matter of case studies which makes them invaluable in our attempt to understand the human mind – and, hence, ourselves? Turning that around, however 'unique' such individuals may be, they're always recognisably human, not some alien species that is fascinating but, ultimately, so different from the rest of us that we cannot see aspects of our 'normal' selves in its abnormal – sometimes bizarre – behaviour.

This is perhaps the crucial point. The fact that some other psychologist cannot 'repeat' the case study doesn't invalidate it. On the contrary, the behaviour is likely to be merely an exaggeration or distortion of more commonplace ('normal') behaviour – it's drawn from the same 'pool'.

More like novels than reports of scientific experiments, case studies focus on the details that make human beings so fascinating and so complex. They tell a 'story' which isn't just inherently interesting, puzzling and sometimes amusing, but which is also informative about all of us. What makes them 'science' rather than literature is that the psychologist or psychiatrist explicitly links the story to some scientific theory, which is a formal, objective attempt to understand and explain the behaviour.

While they can be read 'as stories', they aren't told in order to entertain (although they may have this effect). Their purpose is to contribute to our scientific understanding of ourselves, sometimes with important practical consequences (as in treatments and therapies for helping people with psychological problems).

Geoff Rolls, as a psychology teacher and author, reflects these various aspects of the case study in this unique and extremely well-written book. He has selected a number of case studies (including some of the most famous studies of any type within psychology), which many non-psychologists will probably have some knowledge of. Between them, the studies sample an enormously broad range of human behaviours, both abnormal and merely unusual or exceptional. However, the people described don't display behaviours unique to them amongst human beings; rather, they display behaviours in forms and degrees that we don't usually witness, either in ourselves or in others.

Each chapter is a summary of the original case study (as reported in a book or academic journal), and Geoff's ability to condense huge amounts of information into a single chapter and still to tell a good 'story' is an achievement in itself. But he has also managed to weave into the story the theory and related research which make these case studies science. He has done this, I believe, in such a way that both the general reader (who may not have heard of most or any of the studies before) and the psychology student (who may be familiar with them, but almost certainly not in the detail provided here) will learn something about human behaviour they didn't know before. But both will, I'm sure, be intrigued and entertained by the 'stories' that Geoff has to tell.

Richard Gross

Preface

This is a book full of strange stories. To many people, psychology is a fascinating subject and, of the fascinating stories it has to tell, the most fascinating involve the use of case studies. They range from stories of people with no memory to stories of people who can't forget; from stories of wild, abandoned children to stories of child prodigies. Without doubt, these are among the most interesting facets of psychology.

They can also be the most revealing in terms of furthering our understanding of human behaviour. The problem is that we all want to know more than is available in the textbooks. Scientific journals concentrate on the scientific aspects when we also want to know what happened on an everyday human level. What was it like to do that? What was it like to be like that? How did they feel? How did they cope? What happened next? This book tries to bridge that gap.

Important findings in psychology have often been discovered first through one-off case studies. Such case studies always fascinate both psychology student and lay reader alike. The use of the case study method helps bring psychology to life – it gives a human face to psychological ideas.

The approach taken might be called 'literary science' since it involves a mixture of literature and science. The case studies are told as human stories but, at the same time, the scientific and psychological aspects of each are dealt with.

Students of psychology will recognise many of the stories presented in this book and are likely to want to know more. Those new to psychology will find it a useful and interesting introduction to the greatest mystery of all: understanding the human mind and human behaviour in all its aspects.

Acknowledgements

Writing a book is inevitably an isolating and solitary experience. Nevertheless, there are a number of people who contribute to the process.

I would like to thank Richard Gross for all his support and help with this project and for his willingness to write the Foreword. The fact that he is one of the nicest people you could wish to meet makes the process all the more enjoyable.

Emma Woolf at Hodder Arnold has been an enthusiastic supporter of the book. I am lucky, indeed, to work with such a knowledgeable and enthusiastic publisher. Not only that, her strange sense of humour means that she understands some of my jokes. As with previous books, Jo Lincoln has also helped enormously in all aspects of the final product. Thanks also to Richard Augustus for supplying his brain for the excellent cover!

Work colleagues have been supportive throughout. Special mention should be given to Alex Banks, Andy Pond, Judith Munro, Beth Halford, Michelle White and Shaunie Brett. Pat and Brian Murphy suggested many worthwhile improvements. A career in publishing beckons! Hilary Carr helped locate some of the more difficult research papers. Thanks also to Dr Roger Ingham for his input and friendship over so many years.

The writing of the book has inevitably meant hours 'hidden away' from my family. My partner, Eve, above all others, has been incredibly supportive throughout. Her willingness to read, discuss and offer suggestions on chapters has been invaluable. In all respects, she is invaluable. My children, Billy and Ella, have also allowed me time on 'their' computer and remain a constant source of pride, amusement and fun.

Having read the case study material in great depth I am filled with a sense of awe for what humans can achieve, often in the face of extreme adversity. I acknowledge the remarkable lives of all the individuals documented in the book.

Being human, there will be mistakes in the book and they are, of course, entirely down to me.

Introduction

Psychologists continue to argue about the scientific status of psychology. There's little doubt that scientific findings tend to be given greater credence than hearsay or subjective experience. However, when it comes to the human mind and behaviour, it can be difficult to conduct scientifically controlled experiments that don't break ethical and moral boundaries. This is where the use of case studies can be particularly useful. They enable the scientist to investigate avenues of the mind and behaviour that are not ordinarily available. By exploring the extraordinary we can learn much about the ordinary.

The use of the case study method in psychology has a long tradition. Indeed it is one of the very earliest methods, and Itard's first report on the 'Enfant Sauvage' dates back to 1801 (see Chapter 12). Over the years, numerous books have been published that offer unique insights into people's unusual deficits or excesses. However, these books tend to be written by neurologists and the case studies relate to patients they've come across in the course of their medical careers. This book is different in that it provides more detail on the most famous case studies in psychology – the studies that are referred to in many psychology textbooks. Of course, entire books and numerous papers have been written about some of the more famous ones, but here each chapter is condensed into a more easily digestible 'chunk' dealing with the most interesting and revealing aspects of each case. In addition to the scientific importance of each case study, the human aspect of each person's experience is included. The hope is that we will begin to understand the people presented in the case studies as humans with a unique ability or difficulty rather than merely as 'scientific case studies'.

Luria outlines two contrasting approaches to the study of human behaviour. He calls these 'classical' and 'romantic' science.[1] Classical science has the aim of formulating 'abstract general laws', which can result in the 'reduction of living reality with all its richness of detail to abstract schema'. He notes that this has become more and more pronounced with the advent of computers in that observations can now be reduced to complex mathematical analysis. This book seeks to adopt the so-called 'romantic', or literary science, view. The stories presented here have a scientific point and help to illustrate areas of psychology, but are written from a human viewpoint – they are *human* stories.

Case studies are used extensively in law, business and medicine, but their use is less common in psychology. This is a shame since we often seem to remember case studies vividly and they help to humanise science as well as illustrate psychological findings.

Putting together a case study involves gathering detailed information about an individual or group. It would usually include biographical details, as well as details of the behaviour or experiences of interest. Case studies allow a researcher to examine a particular individual in far greater depth than experimental methods of investigation. Case studies lend themselves to so-called qualitative research methods and thus findings are not 'easily' reported in a numerical fashion; written, descriptive reports are often used, and these outline what the person feels or believes about a particular issue.[2] These methods tend to be criticised as being less 'scientific', and thus less worthy, than more rigorous experimental methods using statistical analysis.

Another criticism levelled at case studies is that sometimes the researcher conducting the study may be biased in his/her interpretations or reporting method. This 'subjectivity' means that it could be difficult to determine factual information from researcher inference. An awareness of this does not detract from the stories that emerge, however. Indeed much of the rich detail available from first-hand accounts would not have been possible had the researcher(s) not formed warm and friendly relationships with the main protagonists. This should perhaps be viewed as a strength of the approach rather than a weakness.

Case studies can help shed light on both specific and general psychological issues. They allow psychologists to examine behaviours or experiences that are so unique they could not have been studied in any other way, and permit the exploration of possibilities in human behaviour that may not previously have been considered or thought possible. The examples in this book illustrate these benefits.

Bromley[3] has argued that case studies are 'the bedrock of scientific investigation' and that psychologists' preoccupation with experimental procedures has led to a neglect of this area. Case studies have the advantage of providing greater depth and understanding about an individual, and acknowledge and celebrate human diversity. Because case studies are about 'real, genuine people' they have a special feeling of truth about them. This helps to make them memorable. However, case studies have also been criticised for being unreliable (no two case studies are alike) and their results cannot easily be generalised to other people. But do we always have to find out universal truths of behaviour? Sometimes, surely, it's enough to explore the life of a unique individual.

1. Bruner, J.S. (1987) Foreword, in Luria, A.R. (1968) *The Mind of a Mnemonist.* New York: Basic Books (1987 reprinted edn).
2. There are more quantitative methods for single case studies – these tend to be rather different to the 'naturally occurring originals' we are dealing with here.
3. Bromley, D.B. (1986) *The Case Study Method in Psychology and Related Disciplines.* Chichester: Wiley.

1 | Innocence lost: the story of Genie

One day in early November 1970, a woman referred to as Irene W. sought out ser-
vices for the blind at her local Los Angeles County Welfare Office. Her 13-year-old
daughter accompanied her. Being completely blind in one eye, and with cataracts
causing 90 per cent blindness in the other, Irene mistakenly led her daughter into the
offices for general social services. This mistake was to change both their lives forever.
As they approached the reception desk, the social worker stood transfixed, staring at
Irene's daughter. At first sight, she appeared to be six or seven years old, with a stooped
posture and an unusual shuffling gait. A supervisor was called immediately and
started an investigation. Finally, after 13 years of neglect, isolation and abuse, the
world had become aware of the girl who was subsequently known as 'Genie'.[1, 2]

Family background

A key figure in the story of Genie, and the person who was to spend the most
time with her over the coming years, was Susan Curtiss, a linguistics graduate at
the University of California. Curtiss wrote and published her doctoral disserta-
tion about Genie;[3] as she put it, to 'understand this case history, one must
understand the family background'. It was hoped that, by exploring Genie's
family history, there might be some explanation for the unbelievable situation
she had found herself in.

Irene had had an unexceptional upbringing, with a working and loving father
and a mother who was reportedly rather stern and unapproachable. One unfortunate incident in her childhood had occurred when she slipped and banged her
head on a washing mangle. This caused neurological damage that would later
have profound effects. It would cause her blindness in one eye and make it more
difficult for her to look after herself and her dependants. In her early twenties,
Irene married Clark W., who was 20 years older than her. Although they met in
Hollywood there was to be no fairytale ending to their union.

At the start of the Second World War, Clark easily found work and proved
himself an invaluable employee in the aircraft industry, so much so that he
continued to work in that sphere after the war. Outwardly, Irene and Clark

appeared happy and contented, but at home Clark was later described by Irene as being overly protective and rather confining. She claimed that her life ended on her wedding day. One thing Clark was certain about was that he did not want children. Despite this, after five years of marriage, Irene fell pregnant with their first child. During a stay in hospital to treat injuries sustained from her husband, Irene gave birth to a healthy daughter. Within three months, the child was dead. The cause of death was said to be pneumonia, although it was suggested[4] that the child actually died of exposure after being left in the garage. Their second child died of blood poisoning soon after birth. Their third child, a boy, was born healthy but, due to neglect, developed very slowly. He was helped by his paternal grandmother, who often looked after him for months at a time. In April 1957 the couple's fourth child was born. She survived a difficult birth thanks to a blood transfusion but, by this time, the paternal grandmother was too old to help with her upbringing. Irene and Clark would have to bring up their little girl as best they could on their own. In her first year, during a routine medical examination, their daughter was described as 'slow' and 'retarded'.

A key incident at this time involved Clark's mother. One day, on a visit, she was killed by a hit-and-run driver while crossing the road to buy an ice cream for her grandson. Clark had been very close to his mother and became deeply depressed soon after the incident. The guilty driver was given a probationary sentence. Clark was outraged; he began to think that society had treated him badly and he started to become more and more isolated. He decided that he could do without such a world and that his family could do the same. He left his job and became a recluse in his own home.

Unfortunately, Clark thought that the best way to protect his family was to keep them at home too. He thought he needed to prevent others in an evil world from exploiting their vulnerability. They were, indeed, vulnerable and they were to remain, to all intents and purposes, his prisoners for the next decade. Perhaps Clark didn't realise that he wasn't protecting them from his own evil behaviour, which was far worse than anything they might have experienced in the outside world.

Isolation

By the time Genie's case came to light on that fateful day at the social services office, it was found that she had spent almost her entire life (13 years) in one small bedroom of their house in Golden West Avenue, Temple City, California. For most of that time she had been restrained on an infant's potty seat attached to a chair. She had a callused ring of hard skin on her bottom from sitting on the potty for days on end. She could not move anything except her fingers and hands, feet and toes. Sometimes she was moved to another restraining device for the night, ostensibly a sleeping bag, but one that had been altered to act as a straitjacket. Genie was then placed in a wire cot with a wire cover overhead.

She was actively discouraged from making any sounds and her father beat her with a stick if she did. He would only make barking sounds and often growled at her as a dog might. Genie's brother, under instruction from his father, rarely spoke to her. Elsewhere in the house, her brother and mother usually whispered to each other for fear of annoying Clark. In her isolation, Genie heard hardly any sounds and, unsurprisingly, learnt to keep silent. Her visual sense wasn't stimulated either: the room had only two windows, both of which were taped up except for a few centimetres at the top to let in a little light. All she could see of the outside world was a glimpse of sky.

Occasionally Genie was allowed to 'play' with two plastic raincoats that hung in the room. Sometimes, she was also allowed to look at edited TV pages, any suggestive pictures having been removed by her father. Empty cotton reels were virtually her only other 'toys'.

Genie was given very little to eat: baby food, cereals and, very occasionally, a hard-boiled egg. She was fed quickly and in silence by her brother so that contact with her was kept to a minimum. If she choked or spat out any food, it was rubbed into her face. This regime was maintained by Clark; it is hard to imagine a more cruel and deprived existence for a young child. He told Irene that Genie wouldn't live beyond the age of 12, but that if she did Irene could seek help. Miraculously, Genie did live that long and when Clark refused Irene's requests for help, she decided to do something about the situation. After a horrendous fight, during which Clark threatened to kill her, Irene took Genie and left home. A few days later they ended up at social services and Genie was discovered at last.

Placed in care

During the ensuing investigation, Genie was taken into care in the Children's Hospital of Los Angeles, in California. Her parents were charged with wilful abuse of a minor and were due in court on 20 November 1970. That morning, Clark took his Smith & Wesson and fired a bullet clean through his right temple. He left two suicide notes: one explained where the police could find his son, the other simply read, 'The world will never understand.' Irene was already in court when she heard the news. She pleaded not guilty on the grounds that she had been forced to act the way she did by an abusive husband; her plea was accepted. It seemed that, at last, Genie and Irene could begin life again.

Genie was examined at the hospital and treated for severe malnutrition. At 13 years old, she weighed only 59 pounds and was just 54 inches tall. She was incontinent and couldn't chew solid food. She couldn't swallow properly, salivated excessively and spat constantly. Her clothes were often covered in spittle and she often urinated when excited. This meant that she usually smelt bad. In addition, she could not focus her eyes beyond 12 feet. What need was there for her eyes to focus beyond the distance of the world she had known in her bedroom? She had two sets of teeth and her hair was extremely thin. She walked with great difficulty and could not extend her limbs properly. She did not seem to feel heat or cold. She never cried and could barely talk. Although she could understand some words, such as 'Mother', 'blue', 'walk' and 'door', she could only say a few negatives, which were rolled into one word, such as 'stopit' and 'nomore'.

Testing times

James Kent, the psychologist at the Children's Hospital, began an assessment of Genie's cognitive and emotional abilities. He stated that 'she is the most profoundly damaged child I've ever seen … Genie's life is a wasteland'.[5] Due to her lack of speech, it was incredibly difficult to assess her intellect. She seemed capable of expressing only a few emotions, such as fear, anger and, surprisingly, laughter. However, her anger was always expressed inwardly – she would scratch her face and urinate, but never make a sound.

Nevertheless, Genie made rapid progress. Even by her third day in the hospital, she was helping to dress herself and using the toilet. A few months later, she made hitting gestures at a girl in the rehabilitation centre who was wearing a dress that she had worn previously. Her observers were pleased to note that this was the first instance of her directing anger outwards. She was also hoarding various objects such as books, and seemed to be developing a sense of self.

A month later, when Kent was leaving after one of their sessions, Genie held his hand in order to stop him. She seemed to be developing friendships with some of her adult helpers.

Genie was subjected to various intelligence tests and she showed amazing improvements over the first few months. In some areas, she gained a year in development over a couple of months. However, there was a 'scatter' in her development – some things she did well, others badly. Her level of language acquisition remained extremely poor, but she had started to engage in play with others and no longer shrank from physical contact. She was able to bathe herself to the same level as a nine-year-old, yet her chewing of food was at the level of a one-year-old.

She enjoyed going on day trips from the hospital. To Genie, everything was new and exciting. Generally, the people she met were very friendly. She was given gifts by complete strangers. Curtiss hints that she felt that Genie was a powerful non-verbal communicator. Indeed, Curtiss became convinced that she was witnessing in Genie unspoken communication – a kind of telepathy.

Genie particularly liked shopping, and collected 23 plastic beach buckets of different colours, which she kept by her bed. Anything plastic was coveted. It's believed that this obsession dated back to the two plastic raincoats in her bedroom. These were her major source of play; perhaps she continued to associate plastic with play.

She had also developed the idea of object permanence: the concept that something exists even when it is unseen (according to Jean Piaget, the researcher into developmental psychology, children usually develop this awareness at the end of the sensorimotor stage of development, at about the age of two). In addition, she was capable of deferred imitation – that is, the ability to imitate behaviour that has been seen before. She showed this once by barking like a dog she had seen earlier in the day. Genie was also becoming less egocentric – she was beginning to understand that other people could see things from another viewpoint, that her way of thinking was not the only possible way of thinking. This ability characterises the pre-operational stage of development from two to seven years.

The prize

Jay Shurley, a psychiatrist and acknowledged expert on the effects of isolation, was also invited to visit Genie. He described her as having suffered the most long-term social isolation of any child ever described in the literature. Rather worryingly, he noted that because such cases didn't come along that often, a contest had developed among professionals interested in Genie as to who would conduct treatment and research with her. Far from being a neglected child that no one took any interest in, Genie had become a prize, the centre of a political battle between researchers.

The researchers argued about Genie. Should her therapeutic interests be paramount to those of the scientific research? It was argued that any scientific findings could help benefit deprived children in the future.

Occasionally Genie stayed overnight at the home of Jean Butler, one of her teachers from the rehabilitation centre. During one of these stays, Butler contracted rubella and, in the interests of all concerned, Genie was quarantined at home with her teacher. Butler became very protective of Genie and began to disagree with other members of the 'Genie team' (as she referred to them). There were heated arguments as to the best way to proceed. Butler felt that Genie was being experimented on too much and that the research was detrimental to her rehabilitation. The research team felt Butler wanted to become famous as the person who had rescued Genie from her isolation. Butler asked for Curtiss to be removed from the team and requested that she no longer have access to Genie.

At this time, Butler applied to be Genie's foster parent. In the end this was rejected on the grounds that it was against hospital policy for patients to be placed in staff homes. With no obvious alternative foster parent, David Rigler, a professor and chief psychologist in the hospital's psychiatry division agreed to take Genie for a short period. The hospital's policy on staff – patient relationships was overturned. Genie stayed with the Riglers for four years.

Unsurprisingly, Genie was not the ideal house guest. She defecated in the Riglers' daughter's wastebasket, took the other children's possessions and continued to spit frequently. However, she did take a great interest in music. On one of her frequent visits to the Riglers' house, Curtiss began playing the piano and Genie loved it. She became transfixed by music, but only if it was classical. Rigler discovered that, during her isolation, a neighbour used to have piano lessons; perhaps this was Genie's only regular source of sound as a child.

Genie was enrolled in a nursery school and then a public school for the mentally retarded, where she could interact with other children. She appeared to be blossoming at the Riglers'. She showed a good sense of humour, she learnt to iron and sew. She enjoyed drawing. Sometimes her drawings allowed her to depict her thoughts when her language failed her. On gestalt drawing tests – which involve seeing the organisation behind a scattered scene or a whole picture from numerous parts – she scored higher than anyone in the literature. One day in the summer of 1972, Genie was out shopping with Curtiss. She seemed overjoyed at the experience, and turned to Curtiss and said 'Genie happy.'

Meanwhile her mother Irene had had her eyesight restored in a cataract operation and had moved back to the house on Golden West Avenue. She continued to visit Genie. Unfortunately, she didn't feel welcome at the Riglers' and was only invited there three times in four years. She began to distrust the scientists looking after Genie and felt that they looked down on her. She never accepted any part in the abuse of Genie, whereas many of the scientists questioned her passive role. Irene maintained a friendship with Jean Butler, though, who continued to question the 'scientific pursuit' of Genie. Butler claimed that Genie had actually declined in the Riglers' care.

After four years, a research grant that the Riglers had applied for to continue to study Genie was refused. Genie had shown little progress after the initial few months and very few academic papers had been produced. David Rigler argued that the 'anecdotal' case study nature of his research was at odds with the work of the established scientific community. He no longer had the funds to look after, or study, Genie, and within a month, she was on the move yet again.

Rather surprisingly, she was allowed to move back home to be with her mother. Here she returned to the scene of her abuse. This was not a success. Her mother could not cope and social services moved Genie to another foster home. This was a disaster. The new parents ran their home in a military fashion quite at odds with Genie's experiences at the Riglers' and not in accordance with her needs. In response to her new home Genie regressed. Like her father, she turned inwards and shut out the world. She wanted to control her life and she felt the only way to do this was to withhold her faeces and her speech. She became constipated and refused to speak at all for five months. The new foster mother became exasperated by this and once tried to extract Genie's faeces with a wooden lolly stick. The abuse had started again and Genie had to endure a stay of 18 months with this family. Her life was falling apart, as had the academic research.

During this time, Susan Curtiss was the only professional to visit her. She was no longer receiving a grant for her work, but had obviously developed a warm and caring relationship with her. Eventually, Genie ended up malnourished and Curtiss persuaded the authorities to re-admit her to the Children's Hospital.

Financial wrangles threatened to make matters worse. Genie had been left a small sum of money from her father's estate and David Rigler presented a bill for the psychotherapy he had given during the time Genie had resided with him. This amounted to more than her small inheritance. The case went to court. Although Rigler won a partial award, he claims that he never received any of the money. He later stated that he took these legal steps merely to prevent the state from taking her inheritance. However, when Irene became Genie's legal guardian again and took over her estate, the money awarded was missing.

That was just the beginning of a series of court cases surrounding Genie. Irene became upset that Curtiss had included the label 'wild child' in the title of her book. She objected to private conversations being published without her consent. She accused the scientists of testing Genie too often and in an insensitive way. She claimed that the testing took 60 or 70 hours per week. Curtiss denied this and claimed that Genie enjoyed the tests, many of which were very informal. Both Rigler and Curtiss believed that Irene's friend Jean Butler was the real instigator of the legal suit.

After much legal wrangling, the court case was settled. Irene agreed that scientists could have access to Genie for specific research. Genie was to receive all income from such research and all the royalties from Curtiss's book. Indeed, Curtiss had already set up a trust fund for Genie to this effect. Virtually all the scientists involved in her case appeared to realise that they had failed Genie. The 'Genie team' broke up and its members went their separate ways. Many of them became disinclined to talk about their experiences. Most accepted that although their intentions had been honourable, their methods may have been flawed. One of the researchers, Jay Shurley, went further. He stated that Genie had been exploited by the team. He believed that Genie was an exceptionally difficult, unique case and that no one really knew how to act for the best. There had been no manual for them to follow.

However, despite the court judgment, Irene 'hid' Genie away in a home for mentally retarded adults and never allowed scientists any further access. Curtiss, in particular, was devastated at this and says that she misses Genie to this day. It is reported that Genie visited her mother for one weekend each month until, in 1987, Irene sold the house in Golden West Avenue, moved home and left no forwarding address. From a research perspective, to all intents and purposes Genie had 'vanished' once more.

There have been subsequent reports of her life inside the institution. Jay Shurley visited her on her 27th and 29th birthdays. He reported that she had become chronically institutionalised, she was very stooped and avoided eye contact. She didn't speak much and appeared to be depressed. He described her as someone who was isolated, who had lived in and experienced the world and all that it offers for just a short while, and had then been placed back in isolation. The scientific alias given to her was more apt than the researchers could ever have imagined.

Neurology

From early neurological investigations, it became obvious that Genie performed well on so-called right-hemisphere tasks and extremely poorly on left-hemisphere tasks. Usually, language is a task that is mainly associated with left-hemisphere processing. Each hemisphere of the brain controls the opposite side of the body. This is called contra-lateral control. For example, a stroke in the left hemisphere is likely to lead to some disability on the right side of the body, and vice versa.

In a dichotic listening task, those being studied are asked to listen through a set of headphones to two different messages that are being played to each ear. In this circumstance, the sounds presented to each ear are processed almost entirely by the opposite hemisphere. Using this technique, Curtiss could present information to a specific hemisphere, in order to find out what processing was occurring in Genie's brain. She found that it was processing language in the right hemisphere, whereas there is usually a marked preference for the left. Indeed, Genie's performance on language presented to her left hemisphere was the same as that of children whose left hemisphere had been surgically removed. Curtiss concluded that our brain development is determined by our environment – more specifically, by our encounters with language before puberty.

Language acquisition: the unnatural experiment

The way in which humans acquire language has been a matter of much debate among both linguists and psychologists. There are, broadly, two competing schools of thought: nativists, who place the emphasis on innate factors or 'nature'; and empiricists, who place an overriding importance on the effect of experience or 'nurture'. Thus, language acquisition plays a part in the nature–nurture debate. One way of resolving these arguments might be to take a child and allow it to hear no language at all. Would he or she still develop some kind of language based on their innate abilities? Pinker later stated that language acquisition is such a robust process that 'there is virtually no way to prevent it from happening short of raising a child in a barrel'.[6] Of course, it's obvious that no experiment of this type could ever be conducted but, with Genie, researchers felt that they might have found a 'natural' experiment, one in which the suggested manipulation of the environment had occurred 'naturally'. Her upbringing meant that researchers might be able to test out many of their hitherto untested hypotheses.

The best-known proponent of the nativist position is Noam Chomsky. Chomsky proposed that language acquisition cannot be explained by simple learning mechanisms alone. He argues that some portion of language is innate to humans and independent of learning. Empiricists, on the other hand, argue that language can be learned without any intrinsic or innate ability.

Nativist linguistic theorists believe that children learn language through an innate ability to organise the laws of language, but that this can occur only with the presence of other humans. Other people do not formally 'teach' the child language, but the innate ability cannot be utilised without verbal human interaction. Learning undoubtedly plays a significant role since children in an English-speaking family learn English, and so on. Nativists also claim, however, that children are born with an innate language acquisition device (LAD). The major principles of language are already in place and certain other parameters are set depending on the particular language that they learn. On being exposed to a language, the LAD makes it possible to set the appropriate parameters and deduce the grammatical principles underlying the language, whether it be English or Chinese.

The nativist approach to language acquisition remains extremely controversial, but there is some evidence to support it. For a start, all children appear to go through the same sequence of language development. A one-year-old speaks a few isolated words, a two-year-old can say a few two- or three-word sentences, and a three-year-old can produce many grammatically correct sentences. By the age of four, a child's speech is beginning to sound more like that of an adult. It is argued that this consistency across cultures suggests an innate knowledge of language.

In addition, there is evidence of a universal grammar structure to all languages. Indeed, languages are similar in a number of different respects. Furthermore, there is evidence that profoundly deaf children, with no exposure to sign language or oral language, develop manual systems of communication that mirror many of the features of spoken language. Brown and Herrnstein conclude that 'one irresistibly has the impression of a biological process developing in just the same way in the entire human species'.[7]

Like other innate behaviours, the acquisition of language has some critical periods. Lenneberg[8] states that the crucial period of language acquisition in humans ends around the age of 12. (Remember, when Genie was found she was 13 years old.) After puberty, claimed Lenneberg, the brain's organisation is complete and it is no longer flexible enough to learn language; thus if no language is learned before puberty, it can never be learned in a normal and fully functional sense. This is known as the 'Critical Period Hypothesis'. Lenneberg never took any interest in studying Genie, believing that there were too many confounding variables in her case to be able to draw any firm conclusions.

The concept of a critical period in nature is not new. Imprinting is a good example. Ducklings and goslings, given the correct exposure, can adopt chickens, people or mechanical objects as their mothers if they encounter them immediately after hatching.

Human infants less than one year old have the ability to distinguish the phonemes of any language (a phoneme is a category of speech sound such as /b/ for 'boy'). This ability is lost by the end of the first year. For example, Japanese children lose the ability to distinguish /l/ from /r/, according to Eimas[9]. Any child not exposed to any language prior to puberty would thus provide a direct test of the critical period hypothesis – Genie was one such case. Given a nurturing and enriched environment, could Genie learn language despite having missed out on the critical period of acquisition? If she could, it would suggest that the critical period hypothesis was wrong; if she couldn't, it would suggest that it was correct.

Many psychologists and speech therapists spent years trying to teach Genie to speak. Despite all this work, Genie never really developed language in the normal way. Although her vocabulary developed rapidly she was unable to learn syntactic constructions despite very clear instructions from her teachers.

On initial assessment at the Children's Hospital, Genie scored the same as a one-year-old, seeming to recognise only her own name and the word 'sorry'. However, she showed great delight in discovering the world around her, and rapidly began to acquire and add to her vocabulary. Beginning with one-word utterances, as toddlers do, she soon progressed to putting two words together in ways she would not have heard, such as 'want milk' or 'Curtiss come'. By November 1971 she sometimes put three words together, such as 'small two cup' or 'white clear box'. She seemed to be showing encouraging signs of acquiring language. Genie even reported the phrase 'little bad boy' about an incident earlier in the day where a child had fired a toy gun at her. She was using language to describe past events. This continued with horrific phrases such as 'Father take wood. Hit. Cry' and 'Father angry.' She repeated such phrases over and over again. Children who reach this stage of language usually experience 'a language explosion' where, within a few months, their vocabulary develops rapidly. Unfortunately Genie did not experience this.

Curtiss suspected Genie was lazy, always shortening words or combining them. Genie earned the nickname 'The Great Abbreviator'. Her speech did progress beyond simple phrases such as 'no eat bread' to 'Miss have new car.' This shows that she could use verbs occasionally and, according to her speech therapists, she was acquiring some of the rules of grammar. But she never asked questions, she had great difficulty with pronouns ('you' and 'me' were interchangeable and reflected her egocentrism) and her development was painfully slow, in spite of intensive training using the most advanced methods. Indeed, from this point on her language acquisition stopped and levelled out.

The evidence remains inconclusive, but Genie provides some evidence for the Critical Period Hypothesis. Her case suggests that language is an innate capacity of human beings that is acquired during a critical period between the ages of two and puberty. After puberty, it becomes more difficult for humans to learn languages, which explains why learning a second language is more difficult than learning a first one. However, Genie did acquire some language so she demonstrated that language could be acquired after the critical period, if only a limited amount. Genie never managed to cope with grammar, and it is this aspect that Chomsky argued distinguishes human language from animal language. From this viewpoint, Genie failed to develop language after having missed the critical period. In many respects, the argument boils down to how we define 'language'.

The methodological problem with the study of Genie is that she wasn't *merely* deprived of opportunities to practise and hear language; she was also abused in numerous other ways. She was malnourished and suffered from a lack of visual, tactile and social stimulation. Given the crucial role of language in human interaction and development, it's almost inevitable that anybody deprived of early language stimulation would also be deprived of other opportunities for normal cognitive or social development. Genie most certainly was. How could psychologists disentangle these effects? This proved impossible to do. In the case of Genie there was also the lingering doubt as to whether she had been born with some biological or congenital retardation. Her father emphasised this throughout her early life and the paediatrician who examined Genie as an infant did mention some problems. However, Irene stated that Genie had started to make babbling sounds and produce the odd word prior to her father placing her in isolation, so she might have been developing language at a normal speed prior to the abuse. Of course, this is anecdotal evidence and, as such, cannot necessarily be relied upon. In addition, Curtiss believed that Genie was not retarded. She scored very highly on spatial tests and developed the ability to see things from another perspective.

Susan Curtiss regarded Genie's case as refuting the idea of Lenneberg's Critical Period Hypothesis, that natural language acquisition cannot occur after puberty.[10] Genie did acquire some 'language' after puberty and Curtiss claimed that she also acquired language from 'mere exposure'.[11] However, it has subsequently been reported that Curtiss appeared to change her mind fairly radically about linguistic nativism. She suggested that Genie's case in fact did *not* provide real evidence of true language development after puberty. Separately, both Sampson[12] and Jones[13] detail the way in which Curtiss's discussions of Genie in later publications contradicted what she wrote in her earliest book, although no fresh evidence was available to her and she gave no explanation for her own contradictions.

Postscript

What can we say about Genie? Certainly, her father failed her, the system set up to protect children from such abuse failed her, arguably even after her 'discovery' the professionals who set out to care for her failed her. Although Genie became perhaps the most famous case study in psychology, her story does not provide conclusive evidence for or against the Critical Period Hypothesis of language acquisition. Her case has become a focus of debate about the ethics of psychological research and the potential conflict between the demands of the scientist and the participant. With no definitive answer as to whether or not she was 'retarded' at birth, she was never going to help clarify the nature–nurture debate.

Ultimately, Genie's story can be seen as a catalogue of unfortunate or misguided mistakes. Indeed, she might be seen as the product of man's inhumanity to man. However, her story can also be seen in a different light: despite the abuse, the lack of care and love, despite all the suffering, mistrust and lack of interest she experienced, Genie still reached out to people, touched their hearts, became fascinated by life and demonstrated the true depth of human forgiveness. In her own special way, Genie remains an inspiring example to us all.

1. 'Genie' was a scientific alias given to protect the girl's true identity. It was felt to be an appropriate choice since she appeared to have come from nowhere.
2. For a more detailed account of Genie, see Rymer, R. (1993) *Genie: A Scientific Tragedy*. New York: HarperCollins.
3. Curtiss, S. (1977) *Genie: A Psycholinguistic Study of a Modern-day 'Wild Child'*. New York: Academic Press.
4. Rymer, *Genie*, p. 13.
5. Rymer, *Genie*, p. 40.
6. Pinker, S. (1984) *Language Learnability and Language Development*. Cambridge, Mass.: Harvard University Press, p. 29.
7. Brown, R. and Herrnstein, R. (1975) *Psychology*. Boston: Little, Brown, p. 479.
8. Lenneberg, E. (1967) *Biological Foundations of Language*. New York: Wiley.
9. Eimas, P. (1985) Speech perception in early infancy. *Scientific American* 252, pp. 46–52.
10. Curtiss, *Genie*, p. 37.
11. Curtiss, *Genie*, p. 208.
12. Sampson, G. (1997) *Educating Eve*. London: Cassell.
13. Jones, P. (1995) Contradictions and unanswered questions in the Genie case: a fresh look at the linguistic evidence. *Language and Communication* 15, pp. 261–80.

2 | The man who knew too much: the story of Solomon Sherashevsky ('S.')[1]

One day in the mid-1920s, a 29-year-old Moscow newspaper reporter, called Solomon Sherashevsky, turned up for work as usual and waited for the daily meeting with the editor of the paper where assignments for the day would be given out. Unlike any of his colleagues, but as was his usual practice, Solomon did not take any notes at the meeting. The editor had noticed this before with surprise and this time decided to reproach Solomon. After all, there were often numerous names and addresses given out and Solomon ought to record the details. The editor decided to test Solomon by asking him for details of what he had said. Solomon proceeded to repeat all that he had been told, word for word. This incident changed Solomon's life for ever and was the starting point of his new career as the world's greatest mnemonist, or 'memory man'.

Solomon's memory

The editor was amazed by Solomon's memory, whereas Solomon was amazed that anyone should think his memory was remarkable. Didn't others have equally good memories? He would discover the answer to that question over the coming months and years. Sensing an interesting story, the editor sent Solomon to the local university for some further tests of his memory ability, and that is where he met Alexander Romanovich Luria, a Russian professor who was to spend the next 30 years systematically studying the most remarkable memory ever examined.

Luria started the examination by collecting biographical details. Solomon, a Latvian by birth, was in his late twenties, his father owned a bookstore and therefore, not surprisingly, his mother was well-read. His father could apparently recall the location of every book in the store and his mother, a devout Jew, could quote long paragraphs from the Torah. His brothers and sisters were well-balanced individuals and there was evidence of some musical talent within the family. Indeed, Solomon had trained as a violinist until an ear infection put paid to that choice of profession and he turned to journalism instead. Despite the accepted link between exceptional ability and mental illness, Luria noted no history of mental illness in the family.

Luria began by giving Solomon a series of tests in order to ascertain his memory capacity. Words and numbers were presented to him in spoken or written form and he had to replicate them in the same form and order. Luria started with 10 or 20 items but gradually increased this to 70 items. Solomon recalled all the items perfectly. He occasionally hesitated with his answers, stared into space and paused, but then continued with his word-perfect recall.

Solomon could also report the letters or numbers in reverse order or determine which letter or number followed another in a sequence. This is known as a 'serial probe technique', whereby a list of letters or numbers is read out and then one item is repeated and the item that follows it has to be recalled. This can be conducted as a test of short-term memory (recall duration of up to about 30 seconds). Most people find this task extremely difficult, especially with a long sequence of items, but Solomon had no difficulty provided that the initial presentation of the list was at a suitable pace. This pace tended to be fairly slow, which is the exact opposite of so-called 'normal' participants, who tend to perform slightly better on a serial probe task if the items are presented quickly (for such participants, the quicker the presentation, the less time the items have to 'decay' in their short-term memory). However, with Solomon it was discovered that he was using an unusual system for remembering the items, which was not one based on normal acoustic or sound processing but involved images or pictures. This also meant that, once he had learnt it, Solomon would remember the sequence of items indefinitely, whereas most normal participants would have little recall of the items beyond the few minutes the experiment would take.

Luria began to present Solomon with different memory tasks. Most people find meaningful words far easier to recall than nonsense syllables or trigrams (three consonants with no meaning), but Solomon had no problem with any of them. The same findings occurred with sounds and numbers; all Solomon required was a three- or four-second delay between each item to be recalled. In order to test the capacity of memory, researchers have devised an approach, originally developed by Joseph Jacobs in 1887, called the serial digit span technique. This involves gradually increasing the number of items to be remembered until the participant becomes confused and can no longer recall them in the correct order. If you try this, you'll find that the typical digit span is seven plus or minus two items. However, with Solomon it was Luria who became confused since Solomon appeared to have no limit to his digit span! Indeed, Luria had to give up in the end since there appeared to be no limit to Solomon's memory capacity.

Luria arranged for Solomon to return to the university for further tests of his memory. At these sessions, Solomon could recall perfectly all the items he had learnt previously. These results confused Luria even more, since Solomon seemed to have no limit either to the capacity of his memory or to the durability of the traces he retained. Luria wrote:

> I soon found myself in a state verging on utter confusion. An increase in the length of a series led to no noticeable increase in difficulty for S., and I simply had to admit that the capacity of his memory had no distinct limits ... [2]

Luria could measure neither the capacity nor the duration of Solomon's memory (both of these can usually be tested fairly easily in a laboratory). Even more amazingly, Luria found out 16 years later that Solomon could still recall the items learnt at the original sessions. Luria reports Solomon saying,

> yes, yes ... This was a series you gave me once when we were in your apartment ... You were sitting at the table and I in the rocking chair ... You were wearing a grey suit and you looked at me like this ... Now then I can see you saying ... [3]

These words offered a clue as to how Solomon's memory worked: images were the key to his remarkable memory.

Luria had a problem. He realised that there was no way to measure Solomon's memory capacity. A quantitative analysis of his memory was impossible. So, for the next 30 years, Luria decided to concentrate on *describing* Solomon's memory, to provide a qualitative account of its structure.

Solomon used one particular mechanism to aid his memory. Regardless of the type of information and the form in which it was supplied (words, numbers, sounds, tastes, and so on) Solomon always converted these items into visual images. Provided that Solomon was given the time to convert the items into images, there was no limit to the capacity or duration of his memories. It would typically take him about three minutes to commit a table of 50 random numbers to memory. How was this done? Solomon stated that if the numbers were written on paper, when asked to recall them later he would call up the image he had of the paper and report the numbers as though he was still staring at it. For Solomon, it was as though he was still looking at the items to be recalled. Indeed, he reported that recall was no more difficult for him than it would be for us if we were to look at the same paper and then report everything we could actually see.

Many memory tasks work on the basis of errors made during recall. Such memory experiments are called 'substitution error' studies. Mistakes that are made during recall often provide a clue as to how memory works. It would be wrong to give the impression that Solomon never made any mistakes; although they did not occur very often they were usually of a similar type, and thus offer a further clue to how his memory worked. For example,

Solomon occasionally misread one number for another, especially if the numbers appeared similar (i.e. 3 and 8 or 2 and 7). Such errors reinforce the notion that his memory was almost exclusively dependent on visual or so-called orthographic processing.

When given a list of words or numbers to recall, 'normal' people often recall the first and last items on the list. Recall of the first items is called the 'primacy' effect and recall of the last is called the 'recency' effect. This pattern of recall is known as the 'serial position' effect. It is suggested that the first words have been transferred to long-term memory through rehearsal and the last items on the list are still held in short-term memory. Once again, as with Solomon's duration and capacity of memory, Luria did not record this phenomenon since, remarkably, Solomon could recall all the items, wherever they appeared on a list.

Solomon, it is clear, had a most amazing memory. Indeed, he had memories dating back to childhood that few of us possess. It is suggested that our memories of our first few years aren't recalled because we haven't learnt to encode the material due to a lack of development in terms of memory and/or speech. However, Solomon encoded his memories in a different way and since this ability was innate he possessed it at a very early age. He reported memories from lying in his cot as an infant when his mother picked him up:

> I was very young then ... not even a year old perhaps ... What comes to mind most clearly is the furniture in the room ... I remember that the wallpaper in the room was brown and the bed white ... I can see my mother taking me in her arms ...[4]

He even recalls his smallpox vaccination: 'I remember a mass of fog, then of colours. I know this means there was noise, most likely conversation ... But I don't feel any pain.'[5] Of course, it's impossible to discover the accuracy of these memories, but their vividness certainly suggests an element of truth.

With such an amazing memory, Solomon was brilliant at spotting contradictions in stories, often pointing out things that the writers had failed to notice. He reports a character in the Chekhov story entitled 'Fat and thin' who takes off his cap where earlier it was mentioned that he wasn't wearing a cap. Given his precise ability, one might have imagined Solomon becoming a detective or lawyer. He could 'see' every detail and could not fail to spot any contradictions.

Synaesthesia

Luria reports that Solomon often had difficulty with encoding or processing information if there was a distraction during the encoding process. This included the experimenter merely saying 'yes' or 'no' to indicate whether

Solomon had heard an item correctly. Solomon reported that these words 'blurred' the image in his head and created 'puffs of steam' or 'splashes', which made it more difficult for him to 'see' the items. Later, during his stage shows, coughs in the audience would have a similar distracting effect. It seemed that all information created an image in Solomon's head regardless of whether he wanted it to.

Luria concluded that Solomon possessed a pronounced form of synaesthesia. Synaesthesia comes from the Greek words *syn* meaning 'together' and *aesthesis* meaning 'perception'. Synaesthesia is therefore a form of combined perception where two (or more) senses become intertwined. This means that when one of the senses is stimulated, it automatically triggers another sense that acts involuntarily. For example, days of the week may be associated with particular colours. A student of mine states that 'Tuesday' is definitely a 'blue' day. When asked why this is, most synaesthetes state that it just is! There's no explanation for why the senses intertwine. Other synaesthetes might 'taste' shapes or 'see' sounds, with the same stimuli consistently evoking the same reactions. This is because they are not learnt, they simply occur naturally. Synaesthesia tends to be uni-directional, meaning that one sense may spark off another, but it doesn't usually work the other way round. Since synaesthesia is the crossing of two or more senses, there are 31 different possible combinations of sight, smell, touch, taste and hearing. The most common combination tends to be colour and hearing (known as chromasthesia). Most synaesthetes experience the fusion of only two senses, but Solomon appeared to have had four senses joined. Only his sense of smell did not intertwine with his other senses.

The ability Solomon possessed to form visual images to represent words was the key to his remarkable memory recall. Whenever he heard a word, whether it made sense or not, an immediate visual image was created. He reported that if he heard the word 'green', he would see a green flowerpot; with the word 'red' he would see a man in a red shirt waving at him; 'blue' conjured up an image of someone waving a blue flag from a window. Even nonsense words conjured up immediate visual impressions that he could continue to 'see' clearly years later.

When Solomon was asked to listen to tones or voices he saw images. He reports an example of this when he was asked to listen to a tone of 30 cycles per second at 100 decibels: 'I saw a strip 12–15 cm in width the colour of tarnished silver. Gradually this strip narrowed and seemed to recede: then it was converted into an object that glistened like steel.'[6] Such examples clearly show how his synaesthesia worked. Repetition of the tones months later led to exactly the same images being recalled. Every sound he heard summoned up a memorable visual image with its own distinct form, colour and taste.

Solomon's recall of numbers worked in a similar way. He reported the shape of the number 1 as being 'pointed, firm and complete'; the number 2 as being 'flatter, rectangular, whitish in colour, sometimes almost grey'. In addition, numbers produced concrete images: the number 1 was a 'proud, well-built man'; the number 2 was a 'high-spirited woman', and so on. For Solomon, vision, taste, touch and hearing all merged. Later on in his career as a professional mnemonist, audiences tested him with nonsense words or foreign languages, and even these unfamiliar words produced sensations of taste, touch or vision. These additional bits of extra information helped to cue his recall. Solomon even reported an association with the 'weight' of a word. For Solomon, these sensations were so vivid that he reported, 'I don't have make an effort to remember it – the word seems to recall itself.'[7]

The method of loci

The method of loci is a mnemonic technique that Solomon used in order to remember items in a particular sequence. The method of loci refers to 'objects to be remembered, which are imagined in known locations' and dates back to Ancient Greece where orators would use it to remember long speeches.

A story that is associated with this technique relates to the orator Simonides of Ceos who was due to give a speech at a banquet in the fifth century BC. In order to receive a message he left the building, whereupon the hall collapsed. All the guests were killed and their bodies were unidentifiable. Using the method of loci, Simonides was able to locate the bodies of the guests based on where he had last seen them in the building. Their relatives were thus able to identify the remains. This shows not only how useful the method can be, but how important it is to pay attention to messages!

In order to use the method of loci, you need to imagine a familiar route or location. Solomon often used a street or road in his hometown in Latvia or a well-known route in Moscow such as Gorky Street. Once imagined, the images to be remembered need to be placed at points on the walk. Items are thus distributed at various locations such as in houses, by gates, trees or shop windows ('the loci'). In order to recall the list, you need to retrace your steps and 'see' the items placed there.

Solomon's amazing visual memory meant that he had no difficulty retracing these 'walks'. For him, it was as though he was actually walking along the route. On the few occasions when he failed to recall an item, he explained that he had placed the item in a location that made it difficult to see on retracing the route. Sometimes he placed the items in a dimly lit spot – say, in the shadow of a tree

– and would not therefore notice the item in question. For Solomon, these mistakes were defects of perception (not seeing them on the route) rather than defects of memory. One example of this involved the word 'egg', which he placed against a white wall and then failed to spot on retracing his steps. When Solomon later became a mnemonist he tried harder to place objects in appropriate locations and mistakes such as these became rarer.

Memory performance

When it became clear to Solomon that people might be interested in his memory ability, he quit his newspaper job and became a professional mnemonist, performing his memory feats on stage.

Audiences often tried to catch him out by giving him nonsense or made-up words to recall. Although Solomon found he could do so, all the visualisations that he had to put in place to recall these 'words' meant that it took him quite a long time to process the information. He recalls one of his most difficult performances when he was asked to recall a long series of repetitive syllables (over 50) such as MA VA NA SA NA SA VA MA, and so on.

> ... no sooner had I heard the first word than I found myself on a road in the forest near the little village of Malta, where my family had a summer cottage when I was a child ... The third word. Damn it! The same consonants again ... I knew I was in trouble ... I was going to have to change paths in the woods for each word ... but it would take more time. And when you're on stage, each second counts. I could see someone smiling in the audience, and this, too, immediately was converted into an image of a sharp spire, so that I felt as if I'd been stabbed in the heart.[8]

Despite these reservations, Solomon still managed to reproduce the sequence correctly. Eight years later, and without prior warning, Luria asked Solomon to repeat this monotonous list of syllables and he had no difficulty whatsoever in doing so.

As a mnemonist, Solomon tried to simplify his recall techniques in order to speed up his stage performance. As mentioned, he ensured that the mental images he used could be 'seen' clearly. He also developed a shorthand system for his visualisations: he tried to create images that were less detailed than those he had used in earlier recall tasks. Solomon found that the less detailed images took less time to encode and he could still recall the words associated with them. To deal with the nonsense syllables that audiences gave him to recall, he linked image associations to lots of different syllables. He worked on this for hours each day and became adept at forming images of nonsense syllables. Using such techniques, he could recall words in a foreign language, meaningless mathematical formulae and nonsense syllables.

Luria was adamant that Solomon's incredible memory ability was an innate characteristic – that he had been born with it. The use of mnemonic techniques during his stage performances were simply devices he used to enhance and speed up his natural ability in order to satisfy a demanding audience.

Other associated abilities

Solomon's extraordinary visual memory meant that he could also perform bodily feats using the power of thought. As he put it, 'If I want something to happen, I simply picture it in my mind.'[9] This was no idle boast: he could regulate his heartbeat and even alter his perception of pain through imagery.

To alter his heartbeat, he merely had to imagine that he was running for a train or that he was lying perfectly still and relaxing in bed. These images were so real for him that his body altered its physiological responses. In addition, he was able to alter the temperature of his hands by imagining placing one of them on a hot stove while holding ice in the other. Recordings of the temperature of the skin on each hand showed that they had changed by a couple of degrees.

In addition, Solomon could alter his perception of pain. While at the dentist he would imagine watching someone else having their teeth drilled. This meant that the 'other person' experienced the pain. He could also adapt his eyes to the dark by imagining himself in a darkened room, and could produce a cochlear–pupil reflex by imagining 'hearing' a piercing sound. Despite Solomon being studied at a specialist neurology clinic, few explanations for these abilities were forthcoming.

Memory problems

It's clear by now that Solomon possessed a unique memory. However, there were downsides to his abilities. Due to the abundance of images that were associated with each word he heard, he had to have information read to him fairly slowly in order for him to process the word as an image.

Apparently, many people, on meeting Solomon for the first time, reported him as seeming rather disorganised, dull or slow-witted. This was certainly true if he was read a story at a fast pace, when he would find that the array of images each word created collided with the images of the reading voice and those of any extraneous sounds. The result would be chaotic, a complete hotch-potch of images. So to take in a simple passage of text sometimes became a Herculean processing task. Skim-reading a passage, or taking just the gist of it, seemed beyond him since each word summoned up such a rich array of images. Solomon found it impossible to single out the most important or key points from a text. Each detail in any text produced further images, which often took him further and further away from its central point.

Solomon was also very poor at processing abstract ideas. To him, everything was processed visually. He said 'other people *think* as they read, but I *see* it all'.[10] He often found that one word in a passage sparked off an image and then, from that image, he would move to a related one not associated with the original text. His own thinking would guide his linked images rather than the text itself. Abstract words were a real problem, too, since they could not easily be visualised. For example, he said that it was impossible to see the word 'infinity'. He saw the word 'something' as a dense cloud of steam, and 'nothing' as a thinner, completely transparent cloud. In effect, he could not grasp an idea or word unless he could see it, and some ideas and words cannot easily be visualised. Solomon's torment was to spend many hours of his life trying to grapple with such things, which the rest of us cope with quite easily.

He was spectacularly poor at coping with synonyms or metaphors due to the images that crowded in on him. To him, 'child', 'youngster', 'infant', 'toddler', and so on, meant many different things, whereas a writer might use them interchangeably without a great deal of thought. To Solomon they were processed in completely different ways. Furthermore, words with many alternative meanings, such as 'wear' as in 'to wear away' or 'to wear a coat', would cause serious problems since the image would always be the same despite the different meanings. Often, Solomon would get so bogged down in the detail that he couldn't see the overall picture. It was almost impossible for him to read poetry. Every word would form an image whether or not it was the one the poet intended, and the image Solomon saw would, more often than not, disguise the associated meaning.

Another skill that Solomon was also particularly poor at was spotting any form of logical organisation of material. He did not readily spot patterns that might have aided recall – indeed, he never used any logical means of recall at all. His reliance on images meant that he often overlooked other ways of recalling information. He was once given a number of bird names to recall, but failed to spot the obvious connection between the words on the list, processing them instead as unrelated items rather than all belonging to the category 'birds'. His imagery technique meant that each word conjured up one or more separate images, and these were disconnected from the next word in the list. The same thing happened when he was given numbers that followed a particular sequence. Solomon usually failed to spot any logical sequence. Indeed, he commented, 'if I had been given the letters of the alphabet arranged in a similar order, I wouldn't have noticed their arrangement ... I simply would have gone on and memorized them ...'.[11]

Perhaps surprisingly, Solomon had a fairly poor memory for faces or for voices heard on the telephone. He complained that faces and voices were changeable and dependent on the mood or expression they had at the time. Solomon saw faces as constantly changing. Solomon compared the recognition of faces to watching a wave changing its shape. He claimed that a person's voice could change as much as 30 times a day. Each voice change produced a different set of images for Solomon, hence recognition of one voice was difficult. He was known to become so preoccupied with the sound of a person's voice that he didn't register what they were saying.

Solomon's synaesthesia enabled him to have a phenomenal memory, but the lack of a dividing line between his senses did result in some rather strange occurrences. For example, he reported that in order for him to eat in a restaurant there had to be the right kind of background music playing, otherwise the sound of the music would interfere with the taste of the food. Solomon stated that, 'if you select the right kind of music, everything tastes good. Surely people who work in restaurants know this ...'.[12] One occasion is reported when he fancied eating an ice cream and went to buy one from a nearby stall. However, when asked what flavours were available the vendor replied 'fruit ice cream' in such a tone of voice that 'a whole pile of coals, of black cinders, came bursting out of her mouth, and I couldn't bring myself to buy any ice cream after she'd answered that way ...'.[13] Another example of this concerns the Russian word *svinia*, which means 'pig'. For Solomon this word evoked fine and delicate images quite at odds with the qualities usually associated with pigs. To him, the sound of a word, the voice of the speaker and the meaning of the word would be encoded together; all of these things had to *fit*.

Trying to forget

Unlike most people, who spend time trying to devise strategies for remembering, Solomon tried to devise strategies for forgetting. It became increasingly clear to him that he needed to forget information. After becoming a professional mnemonist, giving several performances a day in the same venue, Solomon found that he was having difficulty organising all the material he had to remember. He developed a number of strategies to try to overcome this.

First, he deliberately tried to restrict the images he used to aid recall. He tried to focus his attention and limit the images to the essential details that he would need to recall the item to be remembered. In effect, he began to make shorthand versions of the images. He still remembered the material perfectly, but he did not need to encode all the rich details that each item would normally evoke. Although this helped, he still needed a way to completely forget material rather than just code things in a simpler form.

One approach he adopted was to mentally 'note' on paper material that he had remembered during previous performances. He then imagined screwing up the paper and throwing it away. However, he still found it difficult to forget. Solomon found that interference occurred if material in a subsequent performance was similar to that presented during an earlier performance. This is an example of 'proactive interference', where older memories affect newer ones. Furthermore, the greater the similarity between the material, the worse the interference. For once, Solomon's memory seemed to work like everyone else's, since interference is one of the accepted explanations for forgetting. It should be emphasised, however, that Solomon did not actually forget any of the material, he merely found it more confusing to learn and recall.

Solomon, then, still needed to develop a technique for forgetting. He realised that many people wrote things down in order to try to aid recall, which, to him, seemed ridiculous. Nevertheless, he wondered if he might actually, *physically*, write things down in order to forget them (rather than just making a mental picture of himself doing this). He reasoned that if something was written down, there would be no reason to continue to remember it. He tried this technique, discarding the pieces of paper he had written on – even burning them on occasion. Unfortunately, he found he could still see the numbers on the charred embers!

It seemed to Solomon that he would be forever affected by his inability to forget and this became an increasing worry to him. Then, out of the blue, Solomon found a method for forgetting that neither he nor the psychologists studying him fully understood. He explained that after giving three performances in one evening, he was worried about interference effects during his fourth performance. He thought,

> I'll just take a look and see if the first chart of numbers is still there. I was afraid somehow that it wouldn't be. I both did and didn't want it to appear ... and then I thought: the chart of numbers isn't turning up now and it's clear why – it's because I don't want it to! Aha! That means if I don't want the chart to show up it won't. And all it took was for me to realise this! ... At that moment I felt I was free. ... I knew that if I didn't want an image to appear, it wouldn't.[14]

Strangely, this technique of deliberately trying to forget seemed to work, although, to this day, no one knows how.

Postscript

What, then, can we make of Solomon Sherashevsky? His life was a paradox. His greatest ability was also his greatest handicap. His amazing memory meant that he found it difficult to forget but, despite this, he could appear slow and forgetful to others. His memory created practical difficulties for him on a day-to-day basis. He married and had a child, but continued to have difficulty distinguishing reality from the images created in his head. He spent hours each day daydreaming, on a journey through his remarkable memory. Although successful as a stage mnemonist for a time, he had many other jobs and never really found a satisfying career that exploited his astounding abilities. He ended up working as a taxi driver in Moscow – one that never had any excuse for going the wrong way! He was always striving to do something great in his life, but probably felt he didn't succeed. However, his legacy to psychology may mean that, in the end, he achieved his goal.

1. Solomon V. Sherashevsky is his actual name, although his surname is sometimes spelt slightly differently. Often, participants' real names are kept confidential and they are referred to by their initials only. In many articles and books, Solomon Sherashevsky is referred to simply as 'S.'; however, since his real name is now well known it seems reasonable to refer to him by it.
2. Luria, A.R. (1968) *The Mind of a Mnemonist: A Little Book about a Vast Memory*. Cambridge, Mass.: Harvard University Press, p. 11.
3. Luria, *Mind of a Mnemonist*, p. 12.
4. Luria, *Mind of a Mnemonist*, p. 77.
5. Luria, *Mind of a Mnemonist*, p. 78.
6. Luria, *Mind of a Mnemonist*, p. 22.
7. Luria, *Mind of a Mnemonist*, p. 28.
9. Luria, *Mind of a Mnemonist*, p. 139.
10. Luria, *Mind of a Mnemonist*, p. 112.
11. Luria, *Mind of a Mnemonist*, p. 60.
12. Luria, *Mind of a Mnemonist*, p. 82.
13. Luria, *Mind of a Mnemonist*, p. 82.
14. Luria, *Mind of a Mnemonist*, pp. 71–2.

3 | The boy who couldn't stop washing: living with OCD

By the age of 14, Charles was spending at least three hours a day in the shower. He had been doing this for years. He couldn't help himself, he just had to do it.

Background

This chapter's opening paragraph is the way Judith Rapoport introduced one particular case study in her 1989 book *The Boy Who Couldn't Stop Washing*.[1] The book is now considered a classic in psychology and was one of the first to publicise the topic of obsessive-compulsive disorder (OCD).

The essential feature of OCD is recurrent obsessional thoughts or compulsive acts. Obsessional thoughts are unwanted ideas, images or impulses that occur over and over again in an individual's head. These can include persistent fears that harm will come to them or loved ones, an unreasonable fear of disease or contamination, or an excessive need to do things perfectly. Such disturbing thoughts manifested themselves in Charles's need to wash himself almost continuously. Compulsive acts are behaviours that are repeated again and again. The most common of these are washing and checking. Indeed, sufferers can often be categorised into 'washers' and 'checkers'. Charles falls into the former group. These behaviours are not inherently enjoyable, but may serve to relieve some of the anxiety associated with the OCD. Other common compulsive behaviours include counting and hoarding.

For many years, it was considered a rare disease because many people with OCD kept their thoughts and behaviours secret and failed to seek treatment for their condition. This led to underestimates of the incidence of the disease. Rapoport's book helped to uncover the scale of the problem. It showed that OCD was far more common than other better-known disorders such as bipolar disorder (manic depression) and schizophrenia. It is now estimated that as many as 2 per cent of the population suffer from OCD; it afflicts males and females in equal numbers.

The boy who started it all

Charles was an ideal case study into OCD because he displayed many of the classic symptoms. OCD is one of the anxiety disorders, a disabling condition that can last a lifetime. Typically, OCD symptoms emerge during the teenage years, although they can occur at a younger age. If a child suffers from OCD during the early stages of their development this can have serious effects on later behaviour. If left untreated, OCD can destroy a person's capacity to lead a normal life. This was certainly the case for Charles.

At school, Charles had been an enthusiastic student with particular ability in chemistry and biology. There had been talk of him pursuing a medical career. However, at about the age of 12, he started to wash compulsively. There appeared to be no reason why this behaviour started, but washing began to take up more and more of his time each day.

Most OCD sufferers struggle to shake off their obsessive thoughts and stop their compulsive actions. Charles was no different. During the time he was at school, he was able to keep his obsessive-compulsive symptoms under control for a while. However, over the months, his resistance weakened and his OCD became so severe that his time-consuming rituals took over his life. Charles was forced to leave school because he was spending so much of the day washing. His washing ritual always followed the same deliberate pattern. He would hold the soap under the water spray for one minute in his right hand and then out of the water for one minute in his left hand. He would repeat this for at least an hour. After washing for about three hours, he would then spend another two hours or so getting dressed.

As with many OCD sufferers, Charles's behaviour was affecting other people's lives as well as his own. His mother was at her wits' end. At first, she discouraged his strange washing rituals, but later, not wanting to see his misery, she 'helped' him by obsessively cleaning items in the house that might 'contaminate' him. She cleaned everything he might touch in the house with alcohol and stopped people from entering the house and bringing in their 'germs'. Charles's father could not understand these behaviours and spent more and more time at work.

Rapoport reports that Charles was a very easy-going boy with a friendly and playful disposition. He willingly sought Rapoport's help since he was aware of his OCD and wished to overcome it. She proposed to study Charles's brain waves using an EEG. (An EEG, or electroencephalogram, allows a graphical recording of the electrical activity of the brain.) Unfortunately, in order to do this, electrodes have to be stuck to the scalp using a conducting paste. This paste is very sticky and was anathema to

Charles; he could not bear the thought of it touching his body. He claimed, 'stickiness is terrible. It is some kind of disease, it is like nothing you can understand'.[2] Luckily, he was eventually persuaded to undergo an EEG; Charles spent the whole of the following night washing.

Why?

Rapoport spent hours with Charles, trying to understand why he had developed his OCD. He felt that he was compelled to do so by something inside him. He did not hear voices telling him to do it, but he did feel some internal and insistent sense of having to wash compulsively. He was aware that his behaviour appeared crazy to others, but he didn't feel crazy. Like many OCD sufferers, Charles showed insight into his condition. He recognised that his obsessions and compulsions were ridiculous, but couldn't help himself. He just felt a compulsion to wash.

Charles was asked what would happen if he didn't wash. He believed that he might become sick or that it would be bad luck to stop washing. Although a bright boy he couldn't adequately explain why his compulsion had started or, indeed, why it continued.

Charles had never met another person with OCD. He could not have learnt it from directly observing others since he was not aware of other people carrying out such bizarre behaviours. So what had caused his OCD?

Cause?

Brain scans of patients with OCD suggest that their patterns of brain activity are different from those with no reported mental illness. For example, OCD sufferers appear to have significantly less white matter, but significantly greater general total cerebral cortex than so-called 'normal' control participants. This finding also suggests a neurobiological cause of OCD.[3]

Nevertheless, there also appear to be environmental influences that can predispose a person to develop the disorder, thus research concentrates on the interaction between neurobiological factors and environmental influences as well as cognitive processes.

Current explanations for the cause of OCD concentrate on biological factors. OCD patients appear to benefit from drug treatments. Charles certainly did until he developed drug tolerance and the beneficial effects waned. This suggests that the disorder has a neurobiological basis.

Treatment

There are two main therapeutic approaches for OCD: drugs and behaviour therapy. These can be used simultaneously, and the approach to be taken is usually decided in a joint consultation between the patient and therapist.

Charles was treated with the drug Anafranil and his symptoms disappeared for about a year. Unfortunately, he developed a tolerance to the drug. This involves a decreasing response to constant doses of a drug or the need for increasing doses to maintain a constant response. Although some of his symptoms returned, they were not as marked as before and he was able to control the amount of washing he did. He found that by conducting his washing rituals in the evenings they did not interfere so much with his day-to-day activities.

Drugs that affect the neurotransmitter serotonin have been shown to be effective in decreasing the symptoms of OCD. Anafranil, the drug used with Charles, was one of the first of these. This group of drugs works by inhibiting the reuptake of serotonin during synaptic transmission. Studies have shown that there is a correlation between increased levels of serotonin and clinical effectiveness. Indeed, three-quarters of patients report some improvement with the use of such drugs.

Behaviour therapy is believed to be the most effective treatment for most types of OCD. It involves experiencing the fearful situations that trigger the obsession (exposure) and taking steps to prevent the compulsive behaviours or rituals (response prevention). Studies have shown that three-quarters of patients who complete about 15 treatment sessions will show significant and lasting reductions in their obsessive and compulsive symptoms. When compared to drug treatments, behaviour therapy most often produces stronger and more lasting improvement. However, up to one-third of people with OCD will refuse or drop out of behaviour therapy. Understandably there is often a reluctance to endure the discomfort involved in exposure to fearful situations.

More recently, psychologists have been adding cognitive interventions to behaviour therapy treatments. Referred to as cognitive behaviour therapy (CBT), this approach helps people change the thoughts and beliefs they have that may be reinforcing obsessive and compulsive symptoms. Together with traditional behaviour therapy, this approach has been shown to be effective in offering hope to individuals suffering from OCD.

Postscript

Charles displayed many of the classic symptoms of OCD. By actively seeking help, he was put on an appropriate treatment programme that helped to reduce many of his symptoms. He was able to resume a more normal life. The publication of his case study in 1989 also had the effect of bringing OCD to the attention of the public. Many other OCD sufferers suddenly recognised that they were not alone; they became less secretive, sought treatment and have in turn helped contribute to our increasing knowledge of this area.

1. Rapoport, J. (1989) *The Boy Who Couldn't Stop Washing.* New York: Signet.
2. Rapoport, *Boy Who Couldn't Stop*, p. 92.
3. Jenike, M.A. *et al.* (1996) Cerebral structural abnormalities in obsessive-compulsive disorder. A quantitative morphometric magnetic resonance imaging study. *Archives of General Psychiatry* 53(7), pp. 625–32.

4 | The girl who cried murder: the story of Kitty Genovese

On 13 March 1964, 28-year-old Catherine Genovese began the walk back to her apartment after work. There was nothing unusual in that, except that it was to be her last walk. She was stabbed by an unknown assailant, and murdered after having been sexually assaulted. Such terrible occurrences are not unknown in New York City, but this particular crime was to send shock waves around the world. Her horrific ordeal had lasted half an hour and had been witnessed by 38 neighbours; during this time no one had called the police. The case of 'Kitty' Genovese (as she was known) is regarded as the catalyst for research into the phenomenon of bystander behaviour. To this day psychologists still debate the causes of what is sometimes known as 'Genovese syndrome'.

As New York psychology professor Stanley Milgram commented, 'The case touched on a fundamental issue of the human condition ... If we need help, will those around us stand around and let us be destroyed or will they come to our aid?'

The murder

Leaving her job as a bar manager in the early hours of the morning, Kitty parked her red Fiat in the car park near to her apartment. She lived in Kew Gardens, a relatively crime-free, middle-class area in the Queens district of New York. On the short walk to her front door, she noticed a figure walking towards her. The assailant later testified that she immediately started running away from him. She must have spotted the knife in his hand and tried to reach a nearby police phone box that linked directly to the 112th Precinct. The assailant ran and grabbed her, stabbing her several times in the back. Kitty screamed out, 'Oh my God! He stabbed me! Please help me! Please help me!' At this point, many neighbours turned on their lights. Irene Frost heard Kitty's screams clearly and could see the tussle going on. Irene reported, 'There was another shriek and she was lying down crying out.' On the seventh floor, Robert Mozer opened his window, saw the struggle too, and yelled out 'Hey, let that girl alone!' The attacker heard his shouts and hurried away. Unfortunately, that was not the end of her ordeal.

Kitty, although bleeding badly, managed to stagger to the side of her apartment block. She tried a locked door. She looked up to see her assailant had returned. He stabbed her again and once more Kitty shouted out, 'I'm dying! I'm dying!' Again, many of her neighbours heard her screams. Lights went on again in the apartments and a number of windows were opened. A French girl, Andre Picq, who lived on the second floor, heard the screams and looked out to see the assailant lying on top of Kitty, beating her. On the sixth floor, Marjorie and Samuel Koshkin also witnessed the attack. They saw the assailant run to his car, but noticed that he was still prowling around five minutes later.

Once again, Kitty tried to reach the safety of her apartment building. She entered the lobby, but the assailant returned a final time. As he recalled later, 'I came back because I knew I'd not finished what I set out to do.' He followed the trail of blood to where Kitty lay, sexually assaulted her, then stabbed her again and killed her. In all, the attack had lasted 32 minutes. During this time, none of the witnesses had telephoned the police.

The assailant rushed back to his car and fled the scene. A few blocks away, while waiting at a red light, he noticed that the driver in the car next to him was asleep. He got out of his own car, woke the driver and warned him about the dangers of falling asleep at the wheel. A surprisingly altruistic act from someone who still had blood on their hands.

Kitty Genovese's, as it turned out, had been his third murder.

The assailant: Winston Moseley

A week later, 29-year-old Winston Moseley, a manual worker, was arrested for murder. He had no previous convictions, and lived with his wife and two children nearby. Under police interrogation he soon confessed to the murder, saying that he'd had an uncontrollable urge to kill. His case went to trial three months later. Despite pleading guilty on the grounds of insanity, on 11 June 1964 Winston Moseley was sentenced to death by electric chair. However, the judge had made a mistake by not allowing evidence regarding Moseley's mental health to be presented at a pre-trial hearing. As a result, his sentence was commuted to life imprisonment.

A year later, Moseley attempted a prison breakout. He assaulted a prison guard, stole his gun and held five civilians hostage. He raped one of the women and eventually gave himself up after a half-hour stand-off with armed FBI agents. Moseley remains in Great Meadow State Prison, NY, to this day. So far, all his applications for parole have been refused.

The details of this crime were horrific and caused a sensation in their day. However, the sensational story reported in the newspapers did not concern itself as much with the actual details of the murder as the fact that as many as 38 people in the neighbourhood had witnessed Kitty's assault and during that time not one of them had called the police. By the time one person did call the police, Kitty was already dead. It is reported that they arrived within two minutes of receiving the call. The man who did finally call them only did so after ringing a friend in Nassau County for advice. His friend told him to ring the police. Even then, he popped next door to a female neighbour and asked her to make the call. He explained later that he hadn't wanted to get involved.

Had any of the witnesses rung the police as soon as they were aware of the incident there seems little doubt that Kitty Genovese would still be alive today. The question everyone was asking was, 'Why had no one called the police when what they had seen was clearly an innocent woman being murdered?'

Too many witnesses to help?

Soon after this crime, many experts tried to explain the apathy of the bystanders. Numerous suggestions were put forward. These included the alienation of the individual (deindividuation) due to a lack of community feeling inherent in city living. Indeed, in subsequent years, there would be reports of crowds 'baiting' suicide victims to jump. On one occasion, when police talked down a potential suicide victim, they were booed by onlookers. Ironically, a theologian asked to remain anonymous when he stated that depersonalisation in the city had gone further than could ever have been imagined! Many of the explanations remained mere conjecture, so two New York-based psychology professors decided to research the area of bystander behaviour. Their interest in this area of research arose as a direct result of the Kitty Genovese murder. Their names were Bibb Latané and John Darley.

Latané and Darley wondered whether it was precisely because there were so many witnesses to the murder that no one had helped. The first explanation they proposed was labelled 'pluralistic ignorance'. This idea suggested that, in ambiguous situations, people look to others for help and guidance as to what to do (this was said to be the 'social reality'). In an emergency situation, if all the other bystanders are also uncertain and looking for guidance, then looking to others can produce the wrong guidance, sometimes resulting in no action at all. Perhaps the other witnesses looked for signs of action in the other apartments, saw none and so simply didn't interpret what was happening as an emergency. Put simply, if no one else is helping, then perhaps it isn't really an emergency; alternative explanations are sought, such as 'a lover's tiff' or 'just a couple larking around', to write off what has been seen. A French witness, Madeleine

Hartmann, later admitted that she might have misinterpreted the incident and not thought of it as an emergency. She reported that 'So many, many times in the night, I heard screaming. I'm not the police and my English speaking is not perfect.'

The second explanation proposed by Latané and Darley again relates to the number of witnesses present. They suggested that the presence of other people can influence the decision-making process. If there are lots of people present, then a so-called 'diffusion of responsibility' occurs whereby each person feels less responsible for dealing with the emergency. In essence they feel that 'someone else can help'. Given the large number of witnesses in the Genovese case, and the fact that people knew there were many others watching the events unfold (they could see lights on and people at their windows), it could have been the case that each witness believed that others would take responsibility. Each perhaps assumed that another witness would call the police. In any case, if no one helped, then it wouldn't be entirely their fault. They could always say, 'Well, don't blame me. No one else did anything either!'

The diffusion of responsibility explanation was supported by the testimonies of the witnesses. Mr Koshkin on the sixth floor wanted to call the police, but Mrs Koshkin thought otherwise. 'I didn't let him,' she later said to the press. 'I told him there must have been 30 calls already.'

Rather surprisingly, Moseley appeared to be aware of the likelihood of bystander apathy. He later reported that he was relatively unconcerned by the shouts from the apartment building. He stated, 'I had a feeling this man would close his window and go back to sleep and, sure enough, he did.'

Psychological research

Latané and Darley carried out a series of elegant experiments where they tested the so-called 'bystander effect'.

In the first, students were invited to discuss 'the personal problems faced by college students'. To avoid embarrassment, the students sat in separate cubicles and communicated via intercom. Taking turns, each student was allowed to talk for two minutes. During the first turn, one participant mentioned that he had seizures when stressed. On the second turn, it became obvious that this person was, indeed, having a seizure. He cried out, 'Give me a little help here ... I think I'm having a seizure ... I think I'm gonna die here ... er ... help.' A total of 85 per cent of those who thought they were alone with the seizure victim offered help within two minutes; 62 per cent of those who were in a three-person group (participant, victim and bystander) reported the seizure; only 31 per cent of those people in groups of six (participant, victim and four bystanders) went to the aid of the victim within two minutes. This is a clear example of diffusion of responsibility: the presence of others meant that each person felt less responsible for helping.

In the second study, students were asked to sit on their own in a room and complete a questionnaire on the pressures of urban life. While they were doing this, 'smoke' (actually steam) began pouring into the room through a small wall vent. Within four minutes, 50 per cent had taken action, and 75 per cent had acted within six minutes when the experiment ended. However, in groups of three participants, only 4 per cent of people reported the 'smoke' within four minutes and only 38 per cent reported it within six. When two confederates joined the naive participant and answered 'Dunno' to all questions they were asked (such as 'Do you think we ought to do something?'), only 10 per cent of participants had reported the smoke within six minutes, when the experiment ended. This is a clear example of pluralistic ignorance: people didn't want to over-react and lose their cool. In the presence of others, we look to them for guidance. If they appear calm, then there can't be a problem.

Pluralistic ignorance probably explains why the Genovese bystanders behaved as they did. Presumably they believed that, since nobody else was reacting as if there were an emergency, it probably wasn't an emergency. Furthermore, even if some of them suspected it might be an emergency, the diffusion of responsibility effect made them feel less compelled to take action. In a group situation, it is much easier for an individual to assume that s/he does not have to do anything, and to hope that someone else will take care of things by calling the police or yelling out of the window.

The Genovese case still poses the questions, 'Why don't we want to appear to have over-reacted in an emergency situation?', 'Surely it is better to have over-reacted than not to have acted at all?' Many people have explained this in terms of fear of ridicule or embarrassment, but why is it embarrassing to be doing what you think is right? Perhaps people carry out a cost–benefit analysis and realise that the potential costs to themselves (time, effort, danger) outweigh the likely benefits. Would these behaviours be the same in other cultures?

Predictable apathy?

The controversy surrounding the Kitty Genovese case continues to this day. How could all those bystanders have ignored her cries for help? Why didn't they do something? Why were so many of them indifferent to their inactivity when interviewed afterwards? Armed with the insights provided by Latané and Darley it seems that the bystanders acted in an entirely predictable way. Entirely predictable and entirely in line with what we now know about social behaviour in group situations. Remember, the fact that the witnesses were aware of each other's presence suggests it was a group situation. Writing in 1985, Shotland concluded that, 'After close to 20 years of research, the evidence indicates that "the bystander effect," as it has come to be called, holds for all types of emergencies, medical or criminal.'[1]

Lessons to be learned

So were Kitty's cries in vain or have any lessons been learnt that might be of benefit to others when they need help? What would you do in Kitty's situation that might increase your chances of survival?

Given the increased knowledge of 'Genovese syndrome', there are some simple rules to remember if you ever require help. The first imperative is to try to overcome the possibility of bystanders being in any doubt as to whether what they are witnessing is an emergency situation that requires their help. For example, you need to make it clear that you have been assaulted and are not merely drunk. You need to be explicit and specific. You need to overcome the 'diffusion of responsibility' effect by singling out one individual for help. It is far easier to ignore a general cry of 'Help!' than it is to disregard 'Hey, you with the grey jacket, come here, this is an emergency. I need *your* help. Ring the police immediately.' You need to take charge and assign responsibility. Once one person helps, the social norm in the situation changes from non-helping to helping. It's likely that others will now perceive it as an emergency and will all act to help. You will have overcome the 'pluralistic ignorance' effect. You will be inundated with offers of help. Make the psychology work *for* you, not against you.

There is another way the case can have a beneficial effect. A few years ago, there was a drunk staggering all over the road outside my house. I lived on a busy road. He must have walked all the way down the road and there was a clear likelihood of an accident. I thought of calling the police, but my first instinct was to figure that they must have received lots of calls already. However, having mentioned the idea of 'Genovese syndrome' to my wife, I called the police. They arrived in five minutes and took him away. The next day, the police returned to thank me. Mine had been the first call that night; they said that they never mind how many calls they get. The drunk had been released unharmed that morning.

A clearer understanding of the psychological explanations behind the Genovese case allows people to be better equipped to cope with life's emergencies. Such an understanding could save your life or that of someone else.

Unfortunately, the Kitty Genovese story does not end there. Every year, there are regrettable incidents that echo her case. In 2003, the Swedish Minister for Foreign Affairs, Anna Lindh, was stabbed in a crowded department store after being pursued by her assailant up an escalator. There were dozens of bystanders but no one intervened to help. 'Genovese syndrome' had reared its head once again.

Postscript

What can we say about the Kitty Genovese case? Perhaps it can be summed up as follows: 'The crime was tragic, but it did serve society, urging it as it did to come to the aid of its members in distress or danger.' Those words are taken from a letter published in the *New York Times* in 1977. It was written by Winston Moseley. Moseley finally showed remorse for his crimes and even gained a Sociology degree while in prison. To this day, Winston Moseley, prisoner number 64A0102, resides in Great Meadows Prison, Comstock, New York State. He continues to apply for parole and his next hearing is due in January 2006. Kitty's brothers and sister have vowed to continue to contest any such release. They bear no grudge against the apathetic witnesses, only the murderer.

1. Shotland, R.L. (1985) When bystanders just stand by. *Psychology Today*, June, p. 52.

5 | The boy who needed to play: the story of Dibs

Dibs[1] stood alone in the middle of the playroom. The five-year-old stared straight ahead, seemingly unaware of the children playing all around him. His hands hung lifelessly at his sides and he remained completely motionless. His only movements were when anyone approached him. Then he hit out wildly and tried to bite or scratch them. Eventually, he went and lay under a table with his head bowed, where he remained for the rest of the session. It was obvious to anyone who met Dibs that he had severe behavioural problems. Although the teachers were affectionate towards Dibs, they found it impossible to work with him. His mother declared him mentally abnormal and retarded at birth. His case echoes that of Genie (Chapter 1), and psychologists were invited to study and treat him. Enter Virginia Axline, a practising clinical psychologist, who decided to use a technique known as 'play therapy' with him. Ten years later, Dibs underwent a series of developmental attainment tests. He was, indeed, abnormal; in fact, he was a genius.[2]

'No go home!'

The story of Dibs begins at school. Unlike most children of his age, Dibs appeared to hate school. In fact, he appeared to hate life. He often stood for minutes on end with his head buried in his arms leaning against a wall. He sometimes sat in the same place all morning, not moving and not saying a word. He would sometimes snuggle up in a ball and just lie there until it was time to go home. Outside in the playground, he usually sought out a far corner, crouched down and scratched in the dirt with a stick. He was a silent, withdrawn and unhappy child. Despite this strange behaviour, his teachers recognised that he actually liked school. When it was time to leave, his chauffeur would appear and Dibs would shout and scream, bite and kick, and yell 'No go home!' over and over again. These temper tantrums never occurred on his way in to school.

Dibs never spoke to anyone who addressed him and he never made eye contact with anyone. He was an unhappy child, alone in what seemed to him an unfriendly world. Despite his behaviour, his teachers had a genuine fondness for him. The force of his personality had touched them all. His behaviour was certainly erratic – most often he appeared to be mentally retarded but occasionally he would do something that suggested a ready intelligence. He loved books and always accepted them when offered. During story time, he would often lurk under a table near enough to hear what was being said.

The school received many complaints about Dibs's disruptive and aggressive behaviour, and the staff arranged for him to have some psychological tests. The psychologists failed to assess him since he refused to participate in any of their tests. Was he mentally retarded? Was he autistic? Did he have some mental illness? After two years of this behaviour, when Dibs was five years old, his teachers called in a clinical psychologist. This is how Dibs first met Virginia Axline. She was to provide the stimulation and prompting necessary for Dibs to overcome his problems.

The door begins to open

Dibs's mother agreed to let him attend a series of play therapy sessions with Axline. These consisted of a one-hour session every Thursday. Play therapy is a specific form of psychotherapy for children. It uses the therapeutic powers of play to help children prevent or resolve various psychological difficulties. They are given the chance to express or act out their experiences, feelings and problems by playing with dolls, toys and other play materials under the guidance or observation of a trained therapist. Through such a process children can sometimes be helped to achieve their full potential. Play therapists believe that play can be a means of acting out 'blocked' feelings and emotions. It can also help address self-esteem issues and feelings of inadequacy, promote anger management and allow for emotional release.

There are two broad types of play therapy. Non-directive therapy involves allowing a child free rein in the playroom. He or she can play with anything that interests them. The therapist listens to or records all the behaviour. This is often done on video from behind a one-way mirror. The therapist uses factual comments on the behaviour, such as 'So you're going to play with the father doll today', to allow the play to develop. The therapist is a supportive presence but does not become too involved in the play process. This is the method that Axline favoured with Dibs. It is also commonly referred to as client-centred therapy, for obvious reasons.

Directive therapy, on the other hand, involves the therapist taking a more active role in the play. Often they will make suggestions as to appropriate games to play and will use the sessions for specific diagnostic purposes. Therapists will often set up role-playing scenarios that might symbolise the child's own life experiences and then work on possible solutions. For example, animal glove puppets can be used in play fights that symbolise arguments between parents that a child may have witnessed.

Since five-year-olds lack the cognitive maturity to benefit from talking through their problems, it was felt that play could give Dibs the necessary sense of empowerment. He was given the chance to take charge of sessions and direct play activities himself. Through play, Dibs would be given the opportunity to overcome any negative feelings and symbolically triumph over the upsets and traumas that had stolen his sense of wellbeing. Furthermore, he could do this in his own safe and accepting environment. But the question remained, 'How would Dibs cope with this new situation?' The key to this healing process would be his own imagination and creativity.

The play therapy room used by Axline contained a doll's house with numerous dolls and toy cars, a sand pit, watercolour and finger paints, drawing paper and materials, and an inflatable doll that, having been hit and knocked down, bounced back upright again. During his first session, Dibs merely walked around the room naming each toy in a monotone. Axline encouraged this vocalisation by confirming what each object was. On reaching the doll's house, Dibs sobbed urgently, 'No lock doors … no lock doors'. He repeated this over and over again. The therapeutic process was beginning.

A boy of exceptional courage

On his next visit, Dibs took a marked interest in the easel and paints. He went over to them and, after staring at them for a long time, arranged six of them in order of the colours of the spectrum. He picked up one particular brand of paint and said that he thought they were the best you could buy. Axline realised that Dibs was reading the labels. He sat down and started painting. As he painted, he called out the name of each colour. He could also spell the name of each colour. It was immediately obvious that Dibs was not mentally retarded.

Axline's non-directive therapeutic technique allowed Dibs the freedom to direct the play himself. She would respond to his questions and promptings, but it was Dibs who set the pace of the interaction and decided on the play activity. Axline decided she would try to be the catalyst that would enable Dibs to uncover his true self. She hoped to give him the chance to work through his feelings in a non-threatening environment and told him that the playroom was his special place to have fun in – a place where no one could hurt him, where he could step 'out of the shadows and into the sun'.

Axline knew the therapeutic process would take a great deal of time and effort with no guarantee of success. However, she hoped that Dibs would reveal more and more of his true self as he began to feel more secure in her company. When the time came to end a session, Axline would often have difficulties with Dibs. He would continue to plead 'No go home' through his sobbing breaths. Occasionally he would scream and kick out in protest when his mother came to collect him. During these tantrums, Axline did not try to comfort Dibs with affection. More often, she walked away. She realised that he had to be independent of her. After all, Dibs would only see her for one hour a week. It would have been even more upsetting for him had Dibs become increasingly emotionally attached to someone who could see him only weekly; his strength had to come from within.

Although the therapy was important, Axline ensured that it did not become a dominant part of Dibs's life. There is a danger that some patients can become over-reliant on their therapists and Axline wanted to prevent this happening with Dibs. Sometimes, she would stop halfway down the corridor and, however reluctantly, Dibs would continue the walk towards his mother. By this simple act, Axline was showing that she had confidence in Dibs. She realised that he was a boy of exceptional courage.

'The rapy'

On one visit, Dibs noticed the sign on the door to the playroom. He recognised and read aloud 'Play', and then looked at the other word. He was trying to work out what this unfamiliar word was; 'The rapy,' he said.

During the play sessions, Dibs frequently chose to play with the doll's house and the sand pit. He often asked for the doll's house doors to be locked up. As part of the therapy, Axline merely prompted him to carry out his own suggestions. For instance, when Dibs asked for the doll's house doors to be locked up, Axline would ask whether he wanted the house locked up. If he said that, yes, that was his wish, she would suggest that he did it, not her. When Dibs declared that the house was locked, she would congratulate him on his success.

Axline tried to avoid asking direct or probing questions of Dibs. This helped to avoid any suggestion of confrontation and cultivated his feelings of security. She recognised her desire to ask straightforward questions, but believed that no one ever answered them accurately during therapy and thus considered them of limited use. Instead, Axline always tried to ask open questions that allowed Dibs to express himself further. She often rephrased what he had said to give him more time to identify his thoughts. For example, when Dibs offered to give her a painting he'd done, rather than accept it with a simple thank you, she would ask, 'Oh, you want to give it to me, do you?' This technique allowed her to keep open the lines of communication and allowed Dibs to expand the exchange if he so wished. This approach also helped to slow down the process and meant that she did not impose her own standards of behaviour on the interaction. Thanks to such subtle techniques, Dibs started, gradually, to come out of his shell. He was beginning to reveal his true self. He was taking control and beginning to enjoy his new-found confidence and freedom. He started to make eye contact with Axline and, more frequently, a smile could be found on his face.

Every week has a Thursday

Axline felt that Dibs was making progress, although she had little contact with his parents or school, so she was unsure whether this progress was evident beyond the play therapy room. Nevertheless, Dibs continued to have profound difficulties. When upset, he would often pick up a baby's bottle and suck on it, seemingly using it as a means of reassurance. Axline also noticed that Dibs used one of two defensive strategies whenever he discussed his emotions or feelings: sometimes his language would become very basic and rudimentary; on other occasions he would change the subject by demonstrating his undoubted intellectual ability in writing, reading, counting, and so forth. Axline recognised that Dibs felt the need to disguise his true feelings and emotions, and was more comfortable demonstrating his intellectual abilities. It seemed possible that he hid his true abilities occasionally because he felt people placed too high a value on them.

One day, during a session, Dibs picked up a soldier and identified it as 'Papa'. He stood it up so that it was standing, as he put it, 'so stiff and straight like an old iron railing from a fence', and then proceeded to knock it down. He repeated this several times and then buried it in the sand. Dibs left it there for the week. Axline noticed the obvious message in the play and, at the same time, was amazed by Dibs's creative and impressive use of language. Given time and space, he would work through his feelings for his father.

It is easy to see the symbolic significance of much of Dibs's play. For example, the locked doll's house could represent all the locked doors he had faced in his short life. The locked door of his playroom at home and the locked door to his parents' love. Such interpretations were never suggested to Dibs and were not a part of the therapy, but it seems reasonable to suggest that they may have represented such things. Only Dibs could know for sure.

As each week passed, it became obvious that Dibs was enjoying the sessions. He would rush to the playroom with a ready smile. He told Axline how much he enjoyed the sessions, saying 'I come with gladness into this room and I leave it with sadness.' He appeared to count the days until his next session. He worked out which day next Thursday was, whether it was George Washington's birthday or the day after the Fourth of July – he always knew what date Thursday was. Wednesday always seemed a long day, before his session with 'Miss A.' as he liked to called her.

So much to say

Axline had had very little contact with Dibs's parents, until one day Dibs's father came to collect him and Axline went to introduce herself. Dibs interrupted their greeting by telling 'Papa' that Independence Day that year would be on a Thursday in four months and two weeks' time. His father was obviously very embarrassed by Dibs and snapped at him to stop his senseless jabbering. He called Dibs an idiot. Dibs looked completely crestfallen and left in silence. Later Dibs screamed and kicked his father, shouting how much he hated him. He reacted so badly that he was locked in his playroom to calm down. This incident was a key turning point in the relationship between Dibs and his parents.

Dibs's parents were scared. They had never really discussed their feelings and emotions with one another. However, this incident forced them to confront their fears and worries about Dibs. They realised that they had failed with him. They had spent their adult lives using their intelligence to protect themselves from emotional reactions and, unwittingly, Dibs had done the same. Perhaps his parents had also been brought up in emotional wastelands. In their own ways, all three of them had tried to use their intelligence as a form of protective behaviour, and this had made them more vulnerable than ever. Dibs's mother and father resolved to do something about it.

The next morning, Dibs's mother rang to arrange an appointment with Axline. On her subsequent arrival, she was obviously ill at ease. She confessed that she had 'so much to say' and that she had carried a 'great burden' with regard to Dibs. This was her chance to unburden herself. Apparently, though, her husband wanted the therapy to stop. He believed that it was making Dibs worse and, indeed, Dibs had seemed to be more unhappy over recent weeks. Axline was amazed: could the obvious improvement she had noticed in Dibs not be seen outside the playroom?

Through her tears, Dibs's mother described the bitter disappointment of falling pregnant. She had been a gifted surgeon and her career had been thwarted. Her husband was a brilliant, but remote, scientist, and he also resented the intrusion into their lives that came with the birth of Dibs. Furthermore, they were embarrassed by the fact that Dibs was not normal. They were brilliant themselves and yet their son appeared to be mentally retarded. They both felt totally humiliated and ashamed. When a neurologist found nothing wrong with Dibs, they decided he might be schizophrenic. However, the one psychiatrist who examined him declared Dibs to be perfectly normal, but his behaviour the result of severe emotional neglect. He recommended psychotherapy for Dibs's parents, not Dibs.

Axline asked about Dibs's behaviour at home. His mother reported a marked improvement in his behaviour since beginning therapy: he was talking more (admittedly still to himself), no longer sucked his thumb and his tantrums were a thing of the past. She described the incident with his father as a rational protest at his father's insensitive remark. Dibs would continue with his therapy. The family had turned a corner and all were beginning to face up to their problems. Axline noted that many therapists do not undertake therapy without the agreement of, or active participation on the part of, the parents. In Dibs's case, this only came at a later date and illustrates that therapy can be successful even without the initial involvement of a child's parents.

The leaf

During one session, Dibs told Axline a story about a tree that grew outside his bedroom window. The family's gardener, Jake, was told by Dibs's father to prune the big elm tree. Dibs leant out of his window and asked Jake to leave the branches that he could touch from his window. Jake agreed and left the branches uncut. However, Dibs's father noticed them and repeated his request for them to be cut. Jake explained that Dibs liked to reach out and touch the branches, but his father ordered them to be cut, adding that he didn't want Dibs hanging out of the windows. Jake had to cut the branches, but gave the tip of a branch to Dibs as a present – a part of the tree that he could keep *inside* his bedroom. Dibs treasured the branch tip and kept its presence a secret.

Jake often told Dibs made-up stories about the garden. He once told him a story about his elm tree. He said that, in spring the leaves became green due to the showers of rain and in summer the leaves provided cool shade. But in winter the wind blew all the leaves away in order for them to travel all round the world. The last leaf on the tree was always very lonely, but the wind noticed this and blew again, and the little leaf was taken on the most wonderful adventure ever. However, the little leaf missed Dibs, so the wind blew it back to the same old elm tree. Jake said that he had found the leaf one day under the tree, and he gave it to Dibs. Dibs mounted and framed the leaf, and every time he looked at it he imagined all the wonderful things present in the world, all the amazing things he had read so much about. Dibs reported his feelings about Jake: 'I like him very, very much. I guess, maybe, he is a friend?'

During play therapy, the child is encouraged to tell stories about their life experiences. Stories may represent a real incident in the child's life (as here) or a made-up one. This can help to highlight areas of concern and may enable them to make sense of a troubling or upsetting experience. Retelling the story enables the child to work through any feelings of fear or anger that may have accompanied it.

'Mother, I love you'

Over the coming weeks Dibs became more confident and relaxed. He reported how much he liked himself. He told of happy day trips out to the seaside with his parents. He still withheld his speech when he wanted to. He knew how much it upset his father and it was his way of coping with any criticisms that came his way. One day, after a therapy session, he ran down the corridor and jumped into his mother's arms shouting, 'Oh mother, I love you.' His mother left in floods of tears.

Dibs was looking forward to spending the summer holidays with his family. He seemed to recognise that the therapy had run its course. He was happy and content. His mother visited Axline once more. This time she came to thank her for her efforts. She also confided in her that she always knew that Dibs wasn't retarded. She had been sure that he could read at the age of two. She had taught him systematically from a remarkably early age. She reported that, at the age of six, Dibs could recognise hundreds of classical symphonies and that his drawings had an amazing sense of perspective. She had painstakingly pressured him to achieve. She thought she was helping him, developing his innate abilities, but this had turned out to be at the expense of his emotional well-being. Perhaps his mother was unsure how to relate to Dibs and had concentrated on the areas she felt comfortable with – the intellectual side – to hide her inability to become emotionally close to her son.

At his last session, Dibs was relaxed, outgoing and happy. All his behaviour was spontaneous. He said a final goodbye to 'the lady of the wonderful playroom'. A week later, a clinical psychologist administered an intelligence quotient (IQ) test with Dibs. (This is a standardised test used to establish an intelligence level rating by measuring a person's ability to form concepts, solve problems, acquire information, reason and perform other intellectual operations.) The average IQ score for the general population is 100. Dibs had an astoundingly high IQ of 168. Fewer than one person in a thousand would have a score that high. Dibs did not finish the reading test since he grew bored, but even leaving it incomplete he had already achieved a score far in advance of his years. He was an intellectually gifted individual who was thriving in all respects. Dibs had come to terms with himself and so had his parents.

It is very difficult to evaluate the success of play therapy. After all, what kind of measure of success might be employed? The therapy with Dibs certainly appeared successful, but what were the ingredients that brought this about? Was it the play activities, the toys, the warm relationship with Axline, the one-to-one contact or merely developmental maturation that helped Dibs? It may indeed have been some subtle combination of them all. This is one of the criticisms of play therapy, that it lacks experimental rigour. After all, it would be impossible to take another child with exactly the same problems and deny them therapy merely in order to determine whether they would have shown any improvement over the same period.

Postscript

Two and a half years later, completely by chance, Dibs's family moved into an apartment building near to Axline. They met in the street one day. Dibs recognised her immediately. He said that his last therapy session had been two years, six months and four days ago come Thursday. He had ripped out the date of his last session from his calendar and had it framed on his bedroom wall. It was a special day. Dibs told Axline that she had been his very first friend. He was excelling at his new school for gifted children. His parents were happy and so was Dibs.

The family moved home again later and Axline lost contact with them. However, a teacher friend of hers, who knew of her interest in courageous children, showed her a letter written to the school newspaper by a 15-year-old, complaining about the school's treatment of a fellow pupil. The letter contained a series of convincing and eloquent arguments. The teacher admitted that the school was probably going to follow the writer's suggestions. The teacher knew the pupil concerned to be a brilliant and sensitive boy, admired by his peers. Axline noticed that the letter had been written by Dibs.

During his therapy, Dibs once said that every child should have a hill all his own to climb. Dibs had had a higher hill than most, but through hard work, patience, commitment and guidance, he had reached the top and was enjoying the view. He had found his sense of self.

1. Dibs was not his real name. He was referred to as Dibs to maintain confidentiality.
2. Virginia Axline subsequently wrote a book about Dibs and the effects of her therapy sessions with him. It is an entertaining, educative and comprehensive case study and forms the basis of this chapter. Axline, V.M. (1964) *Dibs: In Search of Self.* London: Penguin.

6 The man who lives for the present: the story of H.M.[1]

One summer day in 1953, brain surgeon Bill Scoville tried an experimental technique in an attempt to cure the debilitating epilepsy suffered by one of his patients. With the patient still awake, he cut a hole in his head and sucked out a part of his brain through a silver straw. However, as Scoville later joked, instead of removing the patient's epilepsy, he removed his memory. H.M., as the patient is referred to, was destined to become the most famous neurological case in the world.

H.M.'s past

Henry M. (H.M.) had a fairly uneventful childhood. He was born in 1926 in a working-class area of Hartford, Connecticut, the product of small-town America. He was a quiet, reserved and shy boy, who did the typical things of his age, such as going with his friends to the local soda shop and swimming in a nearby reservoir. He had a particular interest in shooting and would spend many happy hours exploring the woods near his home, hunting birds such as pheasants for the pot. One incident that was later seized upon by doctors occurred when he was knocked unconscious by a boy on a speeding bike; 17 stitches were needed to mend the wounds to his face and head. It has been suggested that some of his subsequent neurological problems may have had their origins in this incident.

On his 16th birthday, he was driving to town with his parents in order to celebrate his birthday, when he lost consciousness, his body stiffened and he began jerking uncontrollably. He bit his tongue so severely that it bled; he also lost bladder control. His breathing became shallow until, after a minute or so, the jerking stopped. These are the classic symptoms of a grand mal epileptic seizure. Prior to this attack, H.M. had noticed that he had moments when his mind went blank, but this situation was only temporary.

Epilepsy and H.M.

Epilepsy is a neurological condition that makes people susceptible to seizures (the old name for a seizure was a fit). A seizure is caused by a temporary change in the way the brain cells work. In the enormous network of neurons that make up the brain, billions of electrical messages are fired to and fro; these determine virtually all our thoughts, feelings and behaviours. Occasionally, without warning, an upset in brain chemistry causes these messages to become scrambled and the neurons fire faster than normal and in bursts. It is this disturbance that causes a seizure. A seizure usually lasts only a few seconds or minutes, then the brain cells resume their normal functioning. Epilepsy can be inherited, but it is often the case that no cause is found.

Unfortunately, H.M. was not treated very sympathetically, either by his family or his peers. He was teased at school, and ended up leaving and having to graduate at a different one. On graduation day, his teachers refused to let him collect his diploma on stage in case he had a seizure. His father, Gustave, was horrified to have a 'mental' in the family. He sought solace in alcohol, leaving his son's future in the hands of his wife. H.M.'s plans to be an electrician were abandoned and, by the age of 26, he seemed destined to endure a life of dead-end jobs. He lived in constant fear of epileptic attacks and by the summer of 1953 was having as many as ten minor blackouts and one grand mal (major) seizure each week.

His doctor made a decision to seek 'expert' help from the local neurological hospital. There were two doctors who could have taken on H.M.'s case. One was Bill Scoville, who specialised in lobotomies, the other specialised in epilepsy. Unfortunately for H.M., Scoville took the case.

The caring profession?

When European physicians first started to take an interest in insanity, or madness, in the 1800s, they believed that the mentally ill had lost their reason – the thing that makes us uniquely human. The mentally ill were often treated in barbaric ways, with little or no regard for their humanity. They were often confined, physically restrained, for weeks on end. At that time, doctors were developing more and more 'therapies' that today seem little more than innovative forms of torture. One developed a gyrating chair, another shook his patients for hours on end, and collapsing bridges were made that plunged patients unexpectedly into ice-cold water. The hope was that such treatments would restore patients' sanity by shocking their disturbed minds. Surprisingly, many of these treatments were reported as being effective in improving manic behaviour; however, it now seems certain that the patients were merely frightened into submission. Doctors were becoming increasingly desperate in their search for a 'cure' for mental illness.

In the 1930s the incidence of serious mental illness was increasing, but an understanding of its cause or how to treat it was not. A Portuguese doctor called Egas Moniz had been impressed when he saw how placid a previously temperamental chimpanzee became after having had the frontal lobes of its brain removed. He wondered whether a similar process would work for the mentally ill and suggested that mental illness might be caused by malfunctioning nerve cells. He thought the patient might show some improvement if these were destroyed. Although he had no real scientific evidence for his hypothesis, he started performing psychosurgery on human patients. Using his own subjective, and biased, criteria he declared the operations successful.

An American professor called Walter Freeman enthusiastically welcomed these new 'invasive' techniques and began extolling their virtues on that side of the Atlantic. Moniz and Freeman published an influential book, promoting the use of lobotomies to treat the mentally ill. The number of lobotomies performed in the USA increased from 100 in 1946 to 5000 in 1949. The technique seemed to offer hope where previously there had been none. Freeman seems to have been a rebellious, controversial character. He developed a technique that involved lifting a patient's eyelid and inserting a leucotome (an instrument similar to an ice pick) through a tear duct. He would push the leucotome about an inch and a half into the frontal lobe and move the sharp tip to and fro. He would repeat this with the other eye socket. He liked to show off his 'skill' by performing two-handed lobotomies on both eye sockets simultaneously. Being the showman he was, he ordered his own handmade leucotome to be made out of pure gold. Unbelievably, he once killed a patient when he stepped back to take a photo of the procedure and accidentally allowed his leucotome to sink deep into the patient's brain. Around this time, Moniz was awarded the Nobel Prize for his discovery of the frontal lobotomy (this was later described as the most disgraceful presentation in the history of the awards). Bill Scoville was studying medicine at university at the time, and could not help but be influenced by this new-found 'miracle' procedure.

Scoville was also rather a wild character, known to the local police for his reckless driving in his red Jaguar and for high-risk pranks such as climbing the cable tower of the George Washington Bridge at night. In his professional life, he appeared willing to take risks in the hope of gaining high rewards. Local mental hospitals used to 'volunteer' suitable patients for pioneering operations, and Scoville used to take them on. He believed in the motto of Walter Freeman:

'Lobotomy gets them home.' However, by 1953, concerns were being raised about the effectiveness of lobotomies. Scoville saw his chance. Could he find a new site in the brain that might be the seat of mental illness? Quite openly, he reported in papers that he was cutting new and different areas in the brains of patients (mainly schizophrenics) and investigating the effects. In none of the papers is there any mention of ethics. Scoville reported that there had been no adverse effects except in one case. This is the first reference to H.M. in any medical journal.

Although Scoville had been warned of the dangers of his operations, H.M sat in his operating chair on 25 August 1953. H.M. was awake but had received a local anaesthetic before Scoville started to cut across the skin on his forehead. Then, using a hand drill, Scoville bored two holes into H.M.'s skull in order to access his brain (which has no pain receptors). He pushed a metal spatula in to lever up the frontal lobes in order to access the deeper structures within the brain. (Years later, brain scans would show that H.M.'s frontal lobes remained slightly pushed up and squashed.) Next, Scoville inserted a silver straw and used suction to remove from both hemispheres what was, in total, an orange-sized mass of grey matter. In fact, Scoville removed most of the hippocampus (a small seahorse-shaped organ), the amygdala, and the entorhinal and perihinal cortexes. Many of the functions of these areas are still not fully understood. The amygdala, for example, appears to play a part in organising sensory and cognitive information in order to interpret the emotional significance of an event or thought. Due in no small part to the case of H.M., it is now clear that the hippocampus plays a part in organising memory storage. In a moment, H.M. had lost the ability to encode new memories. He was stuck in the past and the present, but with no future to look forward to.

Bill Scoville had not finished his operation. He decided to place metal clips inside H.M.'s brain in order to mark the edge of the cuts. If the operation was a success, this would enable researchers, using X-rays, to locate precisely where his cuts had been made. However, on the very first day after his operation, H.M. suffered another grand mal seizure. There were immediate fears that the operation had been of no benefit. However, this was not true. H.M.'s seizures did become less frequent and were reduced to about one major seizure every few months. Somewhat fortuitously, Scoville had been partially correct about his hypothesis regarding the spreading nature of the epileptic seizure within the brain. (It's also now clear that the hippocampus is involved in mental illness, since in both schizophrenia and some types of depression, it appears to shrink.) Unfortunately, what Scoville had not foreseen was the intractable side-effect that has afflicted H.M. to this day. H.M. was, and remains, almost incapable of updating his memory. Despite this, Scoville wrote on H.M.'s discharge notes 'Condition improved'.

H.M.'s memory loss was immediately apparent. His mother regretted agreeing to the operation; she was angry with her husband for leaving the decision to her and with Scoville for persuading her that there was a chance it would be a success. Scoville went home and joked to his wife, 'Guess what? I tried to cut out the epilepsy of a patient, but took his memory instead! What a trade!' He displayed no guilt about the operation and, indeed, published papers reporting it. He did at least, however, warn other scientists about the dangers of precisely this sort of operation. He telephoned one of the most famous neurologists of the time, Wilder Penfield, in Canada, to tell him about his patient. Penfield was angry with him and could not believe that he had conducted such a procedure but, having calmed down, decided that H.M.'s case provided an opportunity to find out more about the workings of the brain.

'Waking from the dream'

One of Penfield's colleagues, Brenda Milner, visited H.M. and started a systematic investigation into him. Largely because of her work with H.M., Milner is now regarded as one of the world's leading memory researchers. H.M. had one of the clearest memory deficits ever documented: he found it virtually impossible to acquire any new memories at all, and although Milner worked with him for the next 20 years, she appeared as a stranger to him each time he met her. From the day of the operation, H.M. was destined to live his life in the past. H.M. would often repeat the same material over and over again. He was unaware that he was repeating himself. Milner became fond of H.M., but in much the same way you might develop affection for a pet. She claimed that he had lost some uniquely human quality during the operation, since it was impossible to build a genuine friendship with a person who could not remember you from one moment to the next.

So what exactly *could* H.M. remember? He still had a normal short-term memory. He could repeat lists of numbers or letters he had just heard. His digit span (the number of items that can be recalled immediately in short-term memory) was normal (that is, he could recall approximately seven items). He was certainly aware of what had happened a minute or so before. But beyond this, or if he was distracted, he could recall nothing. He was suffering from the most severe form of anterograde amnesia (this term refers to the loss of memory for any events after a trauma or, in this case, operation). In other words, he was almost totally incapable of forming any new memories. At first, H.M. also seemed to be suffering from retrograde amnesia (loss of memory from before the trauma) but, gradually, he did begin to retrieve memories from before the operation. He remembered incidents from his childhood. He recognised pictures of famous people from the 1940s. Eventually, most of his memories up to the age of 16 were retrieved, but along with his inability to form new memories he suffered an 11-year retrograde amnesia – that is, he could not recall events that had happened from 11 years prior to the operation. It has been suggested that this provides evidence that memories take a long time to be permanently consolidated in memory.

After his operation, H.M. continued to live with his parents, and his mother in particular encouraged him to work to regain both his memory and his independence. For example, he would be asked to go and mow the lawn. He remembered the procedure of lawn cutting and could work out where he'd cut by judging the height of the grass. However, if his attention was diverted halfway through the task – if, for instance, he was called away – he would be unaware that he had been in the middle of cutting the lawn. It became clear that he would be unable to lead a 'normal' independent life.

H.M. has occasionally surprised researchers by reporting a few memories that were encoded after the operation. He has a vague recollection about the assassination of President Kennedy, although he often confuses this with the 1933 attempt on Franklin D. Roosevelt. He has learnt what contact lenses are and reports that 'Magnum' is the name of his favourite television detective. It seems that after hundreds of repetitions he is capable of encoding some new (but often confused) memories. This may be because later advanced brain scans have shown that minute pieces of his hippocampus remain from the original surgery.

Despite his devastating situation, H.M. remains an intelligent and amusing man. His intellectual powers were not affected by the surgery, indeed his IQ test score has risen since his operation from 104 to 117 (the average IQ of the general population is 100). Once, a researcher accidentally locked his keys in the experimental room; H.M. smiled and pointed out that at least he'd know where to find them, something that he clearly realised would be impossible for him! H.M. continues to do crossword puzzles. He spends hours and hours completing them, perhaps because all the clues are there on the page. He can return to them at any time and immediately see where he's got to. He continually tells visitors that he does crosswords, unaware that he is repeating himself. In a reference to his amnesic state and his love of crosswords he declared himself 'the king of puzzles'. He can still read and write, but reads the same rifle magazine over and over again. Each time he forgets that he has already read it.

As with many amnesics, H.M. has developed strategies to try to hide his memory loss. For a number of years after the operation, he worked in a machine tool shop doing menial, repetitive jobs. He could do these so long as he didn't stop or get distracted. If he went to the toilet he would never find his way back. His supervisor used to ask him to collect tools. He would give him a picture of the tool he required and H.M. would usually succeed in locating it. He has also learnt to notice subtle non-verbal cues that familiar acquaintances exhibit. These help him realise that these are people he should know, and then he can act accordingly. However, this has not always been the case. When he returned home to live with his mother soon after the operation, he would invite all callers to the house to come in for a cup of tea. Because he assumed that all callers must be friends, and did not wish to appear rude, he invited everyone in.

Eventually the research on H.M. switched to the Massachusetts Institute of Technology (MIT), and a former student of Milner's called Susan Corkin took charge of the case in 1966. Testing has continued to this day. H.M. visits MIT three times a year for testing.

H.M. has no idea of his own age or the date. He tends to believe he's about 33 years of age and often guesses the year to be about 1930. He is shocked when he sees his reflection in the mirror (but, then, so am I). Indeed, he has been known not to recognise current pictures of himself. When he is shown a picture of Muhammad Ali, he says that it is Joe Louis. He doesn't remember the operation but is aware that he has a problem with memory loss. He is often worried that he may have said something that may be upsetting to others and that he can't remember it. He constantly worries about this and asks people if that is the case. He does seem to realise that his situation can help others. He once said: 'I keep thinking that possibly I had an operation … somehow the memory is gone … I'm trying to figure it out. It isn't worrisome in a way, to me … they'd learn from it. It would help others.' Although cheerful for the most part, Henry does occasionally seem hurt at being referred to as 'a case'. He says that his life is like 'waking from a dream … every day is alone in itself'. He finds it difficult to hold conversations and ask questions because he is aware that he can't remember 'what went just before'. He reverts to telling a dozen or so anecdotes that he has repeated over and over again for the last 40 years.

Psychological tests have shown that H.M. is extremely poor at estimating time. Beyond 20 seconds, he seems incapable of doing this with any accuracy. His estimations are so poor that it was concluded that, to him, a few days pass like minutes, weeks like hours and years like weeks. This may be a godsend for someone in his position since it would mean that the last 40 years of memory loss may have seemed no more than a few months.

His gift to science

One of Henry's gifts to science was the discovery that there are many different forms of memory and that they are located in different areas of the brain. His memory loss involves 'the processing of memory' – that is, the forming, sorting and storing of new memories. This seems to be something in which the hippocampus plays a major role; not only does it file away new memories, it connects them with related memories and thus helps to give the new memories meaning.

It is possible to determine whether amnesics can learn new things without them being consciously aware of it. H.M. managed to learn a number of procedural memories. Procedural memories (sometimes called 'muscle memories' or 'implicit knowledge') involve the storage of skills and procedures. These include memories of how to perform skilled tasks such as playing tennis, swimming or riding a bike. Memories such as these are most easily demonstrated by performing the actual skill. People have great difficulty in describing procedural memories. For example, try describing the front-crawl swimming stroke to someone.

Specifically, procedural memory is now thought to comprise three types: (i) conditioned reflexes, (ii) emotional associations, and (iii) skills and habits. Each of these types of memory is related to a different area of the brain. The learning of conditioned reflexes is thought to be related to the brain structure called the cerebellum. The most famous example of this was reported by Edouard Claparede in 1911. One of his amnesic patients didn't remember him from one meeting to the next. One day Claparede held a pin in his hand and pricked her when shaking hands. Next time they met, the patient again did not recognise him, but refused to shake his hand. She could not explain why but was very reluctant to do so. This is an example of simple conditioning (learning). H.M.'s cerebellum was unaffected by his operation and so it would be expected that he should be able to acquire and learn things in this way, even though he would not be aware of having learnt them. However, conditioning tests on H.M. had to be abandoned when it was found that he had an abnormally high tolerance to electric shocks. He seemed able to tolerate shocks that any 'normal' person would find painful. The exact reasons for this remain unclear, but it is suggested[2] that this must be another symptom of his widespread neurological damage.

Emotional associations, such as knowing when to feel afraid or angry, are related to the amygdala. Much of this brain structure was removed in H.M. and although he does appear to feel fear and anger he is unaware of *why* he feels such emotions. For example, since the operation, H.M. has occasionally shown extreme outbursts of anger. He once broke a finger when he banged his fists repeatedly against his bedroom door shouting, 'I can't remember, I can't remember', and he has threatened to kill himself on at least one occasion. There were fears that he was beginning to realise how empty his life had become due to his memory loss. However, most often, he can't remember why he was angry, nor his actual display of anger. It seems that feelings of anger may arise but he cannot remember why they occur, what has caused him to feel angry – this, in itself, must be a frustrating and confusing situation.

It is still unclear which brain structures are associated with the skills and habits of procedural memory. Both the cerebellum and hippocampus are thought to be implicated. H.M. could demonstrate the acquisition and retention of new skills. For example, Corkin taught him the technique of mirror drawing. This involves tracing a drawing on to paper while only viewing the image of it in a mirror. At first, this is extremely difficult but, with sufficient practice, people soon improve on the task. H.M. showed normal learning ability for the task but on subsequent occasions when he was asked to perform it, despite having improved in his aptitude, he was totally unaware that he had already learnt the particular skill. Later on, he also learnt the techniques of mirror writing and mirror reading. These examples echo the case of an amnesic patient who learnt to play table tennis to a good standard but was unaware of his ability or, indeed, the rules of the game or how to keep score. Another amnesic, a pianist, was taught a new piece of music. Later, he could not recall it but having been given the first few notes could play the tune perfectly.

What is missing in the case of H.M. is his ability to encode new memories for episodes that have occurred in his life (for example, his 40th birthday). This type of memory is called 'episodic' memory. He cannot store memories of the events in his life. H.M. has also lost the ability to learn new factual information (for example, the name of the current President of the United States). This type of memory is called 'semantic' memory. It is clear, then, that the brain structures H.M. lost are not involved in procedural memory but are essential for retaining episodic and semantic memories.

Postscript

So how can we summarise what we have learnt from the 40-year study of H.M.? Researchers found that short-term memory is not located in the hippocampus; that there are different forms of long-term memory; that the hippocampus is not involved in the encoding or retaining of procedural memories; that the hippocampus *is* involved in the formation of new (episodic and semantic) long-term memories; and that personality is not greatly affected by the loss of the hippocampus.

Virtually all of H.M.'s family are now dead. He has no recollection of any of their deaths. When he is told about his mother's death, he grieves afresh each time. However, he does sometimes report that he has a feeling that she may have left him somehow. With his intellect intact, by estimating what his age might be from looking in a mirror (he is now 78), he can deduce that it is likely that his mother is dead.

In striking contrast to many of the researchers that dealt with Genie (Chapter 1), Susan Corkin, who has spent much of her academic career studying H.M., has become his official guardian, looking after his interests and helping to organise various aspects of his life. She has helped him in the nursing home in which he resides to this day and, of course, arranges his research visits to MIT. She has become a valuable adviser to H.M., despite the fact that he can never remember her.

H.M. has always stated that he wants to help others in a similar predicament, and he and his court-appointed guardian have given consent for his brain to be donated to science on his death. This will enable a detailed analysis of his brain destruction to be made. As Corkin puts it, 'His wish to help other people will have been fulfilled. Sadly, however, he will remain unaware of his fame and of the impact that his participation in research has had on scientific and medical communities internationally.'[3] Even this statement raises important philosophical questions within psychology. For example, can someone give informed consent to an event if they cannot possibly remember having given that consent?

People have often pondered what life would be like without memory. Without memory where would the human race be? There would be no language, no science, no art, no history, no family, no meaningful existence. Our existence would be from moment to moment. We would have only our innate reflexes to enable us to cope with the world – a world that would be completely different from the one we know today. Because of H.M. we can answer that question.

It may be possible to view H.M.'s memory loss as a blessing in some respects: it has served to protect him from fully realising what a meaningless life he has led. The case of H.M. is tragically ironic: the man without a memory has taught us a great deal about the nature of memory, and continues to do so to this day.

1. Virtually every psychology textbook makes some reference to the case of H.M. Perhaps the most comprehensive account of H.M. is: Hilts, P. (1995) *Memory's Ghost: The Nature of Memory and the Strange Tale of Mr M.* New York: Simon & Schuster.
2. Corkin, S. (1984) Lasting consequences of bilateral medial temporal lobectomy: clinical course and experimental findings in H.M. *Seminars in Neurology* 4(2), pp. 249–59.
3. Corkin, S. (2002) What's new with the amnesic patient H.M.? *Nature Reviews Neuroscience* 3, pp. 153–60

7 | The man who was disappointed with what he saw: the story of S.B.[1]

S.B. lost his sight aged ten months. His particular eyesight problem was declared inoperable. However, many years later, science had progressed to the point where his sight was able to be restored. At the age of 52, S.B. could see again. He would see his wife for the first time, and everything else besides. He would surely be delighted with this newly restored gift of sight. However, he quickly became dispirited and depressed, and within two years died a broken man. He was disappointed with what he saw.

The life of a blind child

S.B. was born in 1906. He was one of seven children born into a relatively poor home in Birmingham. He became blind at the age of ten months due to an infection following a smallpox vaccination. His elder sister used to take S.B. to his weekly eye clinic sessions in order to have his bandages removed and for his eyes to be cleaned. She reports that his eyes were continually bandaged since they wept so much with an unpleasant discharge. As a game, the family used to test S.B.'s vision and she recalls his ability to distinguish light and to be able to point to some 'large white objects'. With his right eye, he could also distinguish hand movements at a distance of about eight inches. However, for the most part during his childhood, S.B.'s head was covered in bandages. He reported that he had only three visual memories, these being the colours red, white and black. To all intents and purposes, he led the life of a blind child. He attended the Birmingham Blind School from the age of nine and left in 1923 with a good education and the skills necessary to become a cobbler.

During these school years he was described as a good, well-mannered and smart boy, only occasionally disobedient. He started work as boot repairer in a garden shed at his home in Burton upon Trent. All his tools and equipment were provided for him. The quality of his work was reported as good. He led a largely independent existence, yet he earned only a meagre wage compared to his sighted colleagues. He set up home, married and was reported to be a jovial and active person. He was confident enough to cross any road unaided and generally would not carry a white cane when he went out. It was not unknown for him to injure himself by walking into parked cars or other unexpected obstructions on his familiar routes to the pub or shops. He was a keen cyclist and would go for long rides holding on to a friend's shoulder for guidance. He enjoyed gardening and was described as a positive and enthusiastic person who embraced life.

Such was his life – relatively uneventful, but full – until a routine eye examination in 1957 opened the door for him to regain his sight. The ophthalmic surgeon involved, Mr Hirtenstein, tested S.B. and suggested that since he was not actually blind (technically, this means *totally* insensitive to light), there might be an operation that could improve his corneal functioning and thus restore his sight. The cornea is the 'window' at the front of the eye. It should be transparent and allow light to enter the eye. When this cannot occur, the path of light to the retina is distorted and/or blocked, with a corresponding loss of vision. A corneal graft involves removing a part of the cornea and replacing it with a similar piece from a donor eye. Advancement in surgical techniques meant that such operations were now possible and on 9 December 1958 S.B. received a corneal graft on his left eye, to be followed a month later by a similar operation on the right.

A national newspaper, the *Daily Express*, got to hear about this and reported the case. A psychology professor called Richard Gregory read the story and immediately wrote to the surgeon requesting access to his patient. Gregory, who remains one of the world's leading experts in visual perception, and his assistant Jean Wallace were given the necessary consent, and visited S.B. 48 days after the first operation.

Restored sight

S.B.'s first visual experience when his bandages were removed after the operation was the sight of the surgeon's face. The *Daily Express* story reports that he saw a dark shape with a bump sticking out and heard a voice; feeling his own nose, he realised that the 'bump' in front of him must also be a nose and therefore the dark shape must be a face. He therefore concluded that this must be the surgeon's face. Later reports from S.B. suggest that he recognised 'the confusion of colours' as the surgeon's face purely because he recognised the surgeon's voice. He admitted that he wouldn't have known this was a face without the vocal accompaniment and his pre-existing knowledge that voices came from faces. Initially, S.B. did not find faces very easy objects to identify. He described his wife as 'just as bonny as I thought she would be'.

A well-controlled study would have enabled the researchers to examine and test S.B. both pre- and post-operatively, and would have given them more time to prepare various perceptual tests. Nevertheless, by the time Gregory and Wallace met S.B. they were armed with an array of various tests that they planned to use to gauge his visual abilities. They first saw him strolling confidently down a hospital corridor. He walked through a door with no need for the use of touch and they reported him as appearing confident, extrovert and cheerful. He seemed to have normal sight. However, they soon realised this was certainly not the case. His gaze was focused ahead and he did not scan round the room. Only if asked to look at something in the room, did he give it any attention, and then he would peer at it with inordinate concentration and deliberation.

S.B. could name all the objects in the room and could even tell the time from the wall clock. Given that many people with 'restored sight' struggle with such object recognition, Gregory and Wallace asked him to explain why he was so good at identifying objects. S.B. explained that most of the items he could guess from thinking back to his touch experiences as a blind man. He showed them his watch, which had had the glass removed, and demonstrated how he had learnt to tell the time by touch. Furthermore, he said that he could identify letters in capitals because he had been taught at the blind school to identify capital letters by touch. It was noticeable that although he couldn't recognise letters in lower case (he hadn't been taught to recognise these by touch), he could often use intelligent guesses to cover up any such perceptual abnormality. This 'filling in the gaps' of his knowledge has echoes with the case of H.M. (Chapter 6), who also used 'educated guesses' to try to overcome his lack of memory.

S.B. was not so certain about colour recognition. Previous reports suggested that yellow is often seen as an unpleasant colour by restored-sight patients. S.B. complained of the many different types of yellow. He showed a marked preference for greens and blues, and liked bright colours in general. He was disappointed with 'dingy' colours. He found the world rather drab and became upset at flaking paint and any imperfections on things.

S.B.'s perception of depth was extremely poor. He would look outside his hospital window, which was 40 feet up, and believe he could reach out and touch the ground. His estimation of size also suffered from inaccuracies. He could estimate the length of buses correctly, but not their height. It was assumed that this was because he would have been familiar, due to his touch experiences, with the length of buses, but that he wouldn't have had any experience of their height. In essence, his size estimations were reasonably accurate if he had previously known the objects by touch.

There were two objects that particularly fascinated him. Three days after the operation to his left eye, he asked the matron what the object was in the sky. He showed great surprise to be told that it was the moon. He had thought that a quarter-moon would be like a quarter-piece of cake rather than a crescent shape. Again, the moon was an object he could not have previously experienced by touch. He also showed a fascination with mirrors that continued for the rest of his life. A 'regular' at his local pub, he would sit for hours in his favourite seat opposite the mirror enjoying the reflections he could see.

Psychological testing

Gregory and Wallace asked S.B. to complete a number of different perceptual tests. These included well-known visual illusions that tested depth and length perception, perspective changes and colour vision tests. In marked contrast to 'normal' people, S.B. did not seem to be confused by the illusions. In essence, they did not work as illusions. For example, after careful consideration, he declared the verticals in the Zollner illusion (see Figure 7.1) to be parallel. People usually perceive the verticals as angled towards one another (i.e. non-parallel). Similarly, with the Necker cube (see Figure 7.2), S.B. did not see the figure as representing a three-dimensional object, nor did he find that the faces of the cube 'reverse' (after staring at it for a period of time, many people find that the front side 'reverses' to the back, and vice versa).

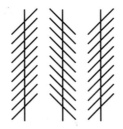

Figure 7.1: The Zollner illusion

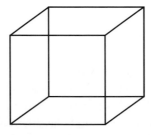

Figure 7.2: The Necker cube

S.B. was also shown a number of pictures of objects and landscape scenes. He was shown one of a bridge over a river in Cambridge. S.B. made nothing of this. He did not recognise there was a river or a bridge. He occasionally recognised colours, but could not make out what they represented.

He was not aware of the concept of overlapping (sometimes called overlay or interposition). This gives us information that an object blocking part of another object from view must be nearer than the partially covered object. S.B. also appeared to have limited knowledge of the concept of relative size or size–distance perception. This refers to the fact that objects of the same size, but of varying distances, cast different retinal image sizes. Hence, objects that appear smaller may merely be further away, and vice versa.

S.B. was given a colour blindness test, the 'Ishihara Colour Vision Test'. This involves numbers or letters marked out in coloured dots on a contrasting-coloured background. S.B. read every single number correctly without hesitation. He had normal colour vision.

S.B. was also asked to draw a number of objects including a bus, a farmhouse, a hammer, and so on. It was found that his drawings were typical of those of the blind. Features that he would previously have recognised by touch were present and recognisable, whereas many features that he could not have previously experienced through touch were missing. For example, his drawing of a bus had exaggerated windows (very familiar objects) but missed out the bonnet and radiator since he had little experience of them. The wheels he drew had spokes since he was more familiar with the wheels on bikes and carts. The drawings always presented the bus in profile, facing to the left, since this is how he would always have perceived the vehicle through touch at bus stops (admittedly, though, most people would draw them this way). The drawings showed that although S.B. could now see the world, he still viewed it through the eyes of a blind man heavily dependent on touch.

The case of S.B. provides very good evidence for cross-modal transfer from one sense to another (in this case, touch to sight). He certainly had the ability to see and make sense of objects with which he had previously been familiar through his sense of touch.

'Tired of London and tired of life itself'

Soon after his operation, S.B. was invited to London to 'see the sights'. On the drive there, he appeared down and unresponsive. He took no interest in the journey despite the unfamiliar scenery. He complained that the world seemed 'drab', and was disappointed when the sun set. He appeared to have changed markedly from the cheerful extrovert he had been immediately after the operation, or indeed before it. He took little interest in the London sights. Trafalgar Square was boring, the buildings were dull and he found the traffic frightening. He lacked the confidence to cross even the quietest road, whereas when blind he would cross the busiest thoroughfare.

On a visit to the Science Museum, he showed little interest in any of the tools or machinery until an attendant allowed him to feel one of the lathes. He immediately became animated and said, 'Now that I've felt it I can see.' At London Zoo, he could correctly identify some of the animals (giraffe, elephant, monkey, lion) but could not identify others (bears, seals, crocodiles). The only occasion Gregory and Wallace ever saw S.B. laugh was when two giraffe heads looked at him over the top of a cage. The trip to London was not a success. S.B. seemed to have no interest in seeing the sights and was generally disappointed with life itself.

Allied to his disappointment with colours and the imperfections so noticeable on objects, he admitted to being disappointed with faces. He stated, 'I always felt in my own way that women were lovely, but now I see them as ugly.' S.B. never learnt to interpret people's facial expressions, and could not use these to determine what others were feeling. However, he could work this out from the sound of their voice.

'Seeing' not to let us down

Gregory and Wallace visited S.B. at home six months after his eye operations. They watched him using his tools for cobbling and woodwork with amazing dexterity. He used machine tools to cut up firewood with frightening speed and proficiency. He confided in them that he found sight a grave disappointment. Whereas previously, as a blind man, he had been admired for his self-reliance and had gained enormous self-respect as a result of his achievements despite his handicap, he now seemed to realise that the gift of sight did not enable him to live the life he desired. Sight afforded him fewer opportunities than he imagined it might. Indeed, in some respects he continued to live the life of a blind man. In the evenings, he would often sit in the dark and not bother to put on the lights.

Neighbours and workmates no longer admired him for his achievements but regarded him as 'odd'. Some teased or tricked him about his deficits, in particular his inability to read. He could see now, so why couldn't he recognise objects and read? S.B. himself realised that though his achievements as a blind man had been admirable, his achievements in the world of the sighted were less so. Maybe he realised what a handicap his lack of sight had been. An intelligent man, he might have achieved much more in his life had he not been blind for 50 years. Although reluctant to talk about the subject, S.B. admitted that he had shown initial enthusiasm after the operation due to his gratitude to the surgeons and those people who had taken such an interest in his case. He was obviously suffering from depression and stated that he had lost more than he had gained from the operation. S.B.'s initial enthusiasm for the operation was attributed to his desire 'not to let anyone down'. Many people had invested a great deal of time, knowledge and expertise in his case, and he didn't want to appear ungrateful. However, as time went by, he could not hide his disillusionment, probably missing the respect and admiration he had earned as a blind man, coping so well.

The relevance of the case of S.B. to perception

As is true of all chapters in this book, it is difficult to draw conclusions from a single case study. In S.B.'s case, it remains unclear whether what applies after the recovery of sight can also be applied to the development of sight in infancy. Psychologists such as Donald Hebb have suggested that the 'crisis of motivation' that S.B. experienced, and noted in other cases of sight recovery, is due to the difficulty in acquiring the perceptual skill of vision. However, Gregory and Wallace argue that it is an *overall* sense of inadequacy that affects patients adversely, rather than the slow pace by which they can learn to acquire perceptual skills. Patients such as S.B. realise they will remain handicapped in the world of the seeing, thus their feelings are more than a simple response to any slowness in perceptual learning. Hebb draws close comparisons between child perceptual learning and restored-sight learning. Gregory and Wallace question this view. For example, they ask why a child does not seem to suffer a crisis at the slowness of perceptual learning and they add that people of restored sight have spent years making sense of the world through touch. This is very different to the child that starts from scratch. Gregory and Wallace conclude that the development of visual perception in the child and the restored-sight adult are very different and few meaningful comparisons can be made. They conclude that the main difficulty with S.B. was not learning *per se*, but changing his learning from a reliance on touching to one of seeing. He had to *unlearn* his perceptual habits in order to learn new ones. This is always more difficult than learning something from scratch. For example, if you have learnt to touch type incorrectly it is much more difficult to change this than it would be to learn correctly in the first place.

With regard to the visual illusion tests, the evidence suggests that S.B.'s spatial organisation was not normal. He did not perceive the illusions as illusions. This suggests that these cues to perception are learnt and not innate and that he had not learnt them yet. It is interesting to speculate as to whether he would have started to see them as illusions over time.

Postscript

S.B.'s health continued to decline. His nerves became worse, his hands developed a marked tremble, he was signed off from work, collapsed on a couple of occasions and was referred to a psychiatrist. With his 'handicap' gone, he had lost his self-respect. S.B. died on 2 August 1960, less than two years after his sight-restoring operations. It is probably no exaggeration to say that he died because he was disappointed with what he saw.

1. S.B.'s real name was Sidney Bradford, as reported in Gregory, R. (1986) *Odd Perceptions*. London: Routledge. Further details of the case of S.B. can be found in: Gregory, R.L. and Wallace, J.G. (1963) *Recovery from Early Blindness: A Case Study*. Experimental Psychology Society Monograph No. 2, and Gregory, R.L. (1997) *Eye and Brain* (5th edition). London: Weidenfeld and Nicolson.

8 | The men who didn't sleep: the story of Peter Tripp and Randy Gardner

Peter Tripp was a world-famous New York disc jockey in the late 1950s. Randy Gardner was an ordinary schoolboy from San Diego. They both decided to do something extraordinary. They would each try to break the world record for the longest time without sleep. Psychologists who heard of their attempts warned them of the dangers involved, but their minds were made up. They both achieved their goals, but in very different ways. Their experiences helped psychologists to discover some of the mysteries of sleep. In the scientific literature, they would always be known as 'the men who didn't sleep'.

Why do we sleep?

Psychologists still don't know the answer to questions such as 'Why do we sleep?', 'How much sleep do we need?' and, more fundamentally, 'Do we really need sleep at all?' One way of answering such questions would be to find an individual who never sleeps but is nevertheless perfectly healthy. Unfortunately, there aren't any documented cases like that and it's most unlikely there ever will be. Perhaps that fact in itself answers the third, fundamental, question.

Another way of studying the function of sleep would be to deprive individuals of sleep and note any effects. A distinction needs to be made at the outset between total and partial sleep-deprivation studies. Sleep may appear to be a single state of rest, but in reality it is composed of a number of distinct stages. These stages can be detected using an electroencephalogram (EEG), which can record brain waves. There are four stages of slow-wave sleep (SWS) and a fifth stage that is known as the REM (rapid eye movement) stage. In REM sleep, bursts of rapid eye movements are detectable and it is at this point that most dreaming takes place. A complete cycle of sleep typically lasts about 90 minutes and therefore, during an average night, a person will experience four to five complete cycles. Using a laboratory situation and an EEG it is possible to deprive sleepers of particular stages of sleep. This is called partial sleep deprivation. Depriving people or animals of all sleep is called total sleep deprivation.

Studies have investigated the effect of total and partial sleep deprivation in animals. The earliest were performed by Marie de Manaceine in 1894 when she deprived puppies of all sleep. She found that they all died within four to six days. Jouvet (1967)[1] devised an ingenious, but cruel, method to deprive cats of dream (REM) sleep. The laboratory cats were placed on tiny islands (upturned flowerpots) surrounded by water. When a cat enters REM sleep its postural muscles relax; this meant that the lab cats lost balance and fell into the water. This woke them up and they climbed back on to the flowerpots and started the sleep-stage process all over again. The cats could go through all the stages of sleep except REM sleep. Interestingly, the cats became conditioned, even while asleep, to wake up when they went into REM sleep, so didn't have to fall into the water each time. The cats become disturbed very quickly and died after an average of about 35 days.

Of course, such findings may not be relevant to human behaviour. The ideal scenario would be to find a human who would try to stay awake as long as possible, for days on end. The first human sleep-deprivation study of this sort was conducted by Patrick and Gilbert[2] in 1896, when they kept three men awake for 90 hours. The participants reported decreases in sensory acuity, reaction times and memory ability. One of them suffered visual hallucinations.

People's willingness to take part in competitions to stay awake has a chequered history. Perhaps the most interesting examples of this involve so-called dance marathons (or 'derbies'). These reached the height of their popularity during the depression years (1920–30) in the USA (however, it is believed that the first recorded case of such a marathon took place in London in 1364). The rules were very simple. Dancing couples had to stay awake for as long as possible and 'dance' to the music. The last couple standing won the cash prize. Prizes ranged from $500 to $3000 – huge sums in the 1930s. Some contests allowed rest breaks and some allowed one partner to fall asleep while the other held them up and continued 'dancing'. The longest dance marathon lasted over 22 weeks! Eventually, such contests fell out of favour and were outlawed in many states in America. An Academy Award-winning feature film called *They Shoot Horses Don't They?*, starring Jane Fonda, portrays this craze.

Peter Tripp

One of the first scientifically observed studies of human sleep deprivation took place in 1959 and involved a very famous New York disc jockey called Peter Tripp. In a stunt that would later inspire Randy Gardner, Tripp decided to raise money for a charity by staying awake for eight days and eight hours. Although this was ostensibly a publicity stunt, some psychologists and medics were given the chance to study the effects this might have on his behaviour. Tripp continued throughout the stunt to broadcast from a glass booth in Times Square, where people gathered to watch. Initially, the 32-year-old Tripp seemed to cope extremely well without sleep. His broadcasts remained entertaining, and he laughed and joked his way through his daily three-hour shows. However, on the third day, Tripp had started to be abusive to colleagues and, not surprisingly, reported himself to be extremely tired. He began to suffer from visual hallucinations (for example, he reported finding cobwebs in his shoes). After 100 hours without sleep, the mental agility tests he was asked to perform became intolerable for him. He saw the suit of one of the scientists studying him as being composed of furry worms. After 120 hours, he went to the Hotel Astor to change his clothes; on opening a drawer, he 'saw' a fire ablaze and ran out into the street for help. When it was pointed out that there was no fire, Tripp accused his doctors of staging the event to 'test' him.

In the last few days of his stunt, Tripp's speech became slurred, he developed an even more acute paranoid psychosis, and experienced further auditory and visual hallucinations. He began to accuse people of trying to poison him, he reported seeing kittens and mice, and questioned whether he really was Peter Tripp. He could not perform simple tasks such as reciting the alphabet, and became convinced his doctors were conspiring to send him to prison. On the last morning, he mistook one of his doctors for an undertaker who had come to collect his body!

Throughout his feat of endurance, scientists had attempted to test Tripp on a daily basis. Unfortunately, in the later stages, many of these tests were not completed since Tripp refused to cooperate with his 'conspiring' doctors. There is little doubt that in Tripp's case lack of sleep resulted in the development of a mental disorder. The doctors described his mental state as 'nocturnal psychosis'. The evidence appeared to show that sleep is essential for normal functioning. Put simply, the body and brain require sleep. Indeed, although awake throughout his stunt, Tripp's brain patterns often resembled those seen in sleep. Tripp gained his world record by staying awake for 201 hours and his 'wake-athon' became a scientifically cited case study. According to his son Peter Jr, 'What started out as a stunt has become required reading in the behavioural sciences at colleges and universities from coast-to-coast.' However, there were two unique factors of this case study that detracted from its relevance to sleep debt research. The first was that Tripp used large amounts of stimulants to stay awake during the last 66 hours of his marathon. The second was that Tripp's experience may have been adversely affected by the fact that it took place on a public stage. His ordeal, and indeed his symptoms, may have been worsened by the use of drugs and the glare of publicity. Due to these factors, many scientists have questioned whether the results gained from such a study can be generalised to a wider population.

After his wake-athon, Tripp slept for 13 hours and 13 minutes, spending the majority of this time in REM sleep. Indeed, one of his episodes of REM sleep was among the longest ever recorded. The phenomenon where sleep-deprived people spend a higher proportion of their sleep on subsequent nights in dream or REM sleep is called 'REM rebound'. It appeared that the loss of REM sleep had led to the psychotic symptoms evident with Tripp. William Dement, one of the sleep researchers involved in monitoring the record attempt, concluded that if people were not allowed REM sleep they would become mentally unstable. Indeed, Dement originally suggested that the results gained from this study provided evidence to support Freud's theory that if taboo thoughts or desires were not expressed through dreams (REM sleep), psychic pressure would build up and lead to psychotic hallucinatory episodes. In summary, he concluded that dreams are the 'safety valve' of the mind and that Tripp had became mentally unstable because he tried to do without them.

With the benefit of hindsight and years of subsequent research (not least the case of Randy Gardner, discussed below), Dement questioned his original position; he never consistently found that REM deprivation caused mental illness. In fact, Dement believed it was far more likely that the amphetamine-like stimulant Ritalin, given to Tripp in large doses to help him stay awake, accounted for his paranoia and hallucinations. Little was known about the effects of such drugs at the time, but now amphetamine-induced psychoses, almost identical to Tripp's, are widely reported in the scientific literature. It appears that Peter Tripp literally went on a 'trip' and that his psychotic episodes were drug-induced rather than caused by a lack of sleep or, more specifically, REM sleep.

Tripp appeared to recover from his marathon and resumed his job as a DJ. However, his career nose-dived and, after a serious of financial scandals, he lost his job in 1967. It is often reported that the sleep-deprivation marathon had a long-term effect on his personality. However, he was very successful in a number of subsequent, diverse jobs and it appears unlikely that the effects of the stunt were permanent or long-lasting.

Randy Gardner

Six years later, Randy Gardner, while wondering what he could possibly do to win the San Diego Science Fair, read about Tripp's sleep-deprivation stunt. With the help of two friends, he decided to try to beat Tripp's world record by going

11 days without sleep. Gardner reckoned that he could do this and, in his own words, 'not go insane'. This case study was also observed by William Dement and would change his mind about the psychological effects of long-term sleep deprivation.

Dement found out about Randy Gardner's world record attempt from a local newspaper. The newspaper reported that Randy had already successfully completed 80 hours of his planned 264-hour ordeal. Dement immediately contacted Randy and his parents, and offered his assistance. Randy's parents in particular were grateful for the medical expertise that was offered; they had been extremely anxious about the consequences that might ensue from such an attempt.

Dement and a colleague, George Gulevich, agreed to supervise and authenticate the attempt. They found Randy to be a cheerful, happy, physically fit 17-year-old, who initially had little difficulty coping with his sleep deprivation. However, this state of affairs slowly changed. During the nights, the researchers found it increasingly difficult to keep him awake. Randy would ask to shut his eyes in order to 'rest' them but not to fall asleep. The hours between 3 am and 7 am were particularly testing. Occasionally, Dement would have to shout at Randy in order to keep him awake. Sometimes Randy got extremely angry and occasionally he forgot why he wasn't allowed to sleep. In order to cope with this, a number of techniques were employed to prevent him falling asleep. Dement and Gulevich ensured Randy was physically active whenever he felt particularly drowsy. They would make him go and play basketball in his backyard in the middle of the night or Dement would drive him around in his convertible with the radio blaring loudly. Randy had to be watched like a hawk at all times to prevent him nodding off. During his record attempt, Randy took no stimulant drugs, not even coffee.

One side-effect of this regime was that the two researchers also became sleep deprived. Indeed, on one occasion, Dement was fined and cautioned for mistakenly driving down a one-way street. His protestations that he was merely conducting a study into sleep deprivation got him nowhere with the police officers involved. Later, Dement recognised that driving while tired is an extremely reckless thing to do and that he fully deserved his citation.

On the last night of the study, Dement took Randy to an amusement arcade and they played about 100 games on a mechanical baseball machine. Randy won every game, which showed that either he had coped remarkably well without sleep or that Dement was particularly poor at the game! Dement recalls that near the end of the ordeal Randy was helped by all the publicity his feat was attracting. Newspaper and television reporters from all over the globe were descending on San Diego to see the world record being broken. Randy found this extremely exciting and there is no doubt that it increased his motivation to keep going.

At 5 am on his 11th day without sleep, Randy gave a press conference to announce he had broken the world record[3] for sleep deprivation. His performance during the conference was described as 'flawless'; he spoke eloquently and there were no obvious signs of sleep deprivation. Randy declared that sleep deprivation was simply a question of 'mind over matter'. He even said that he thought he could cope with another day or two without sleep, but was aware of the need to go back to school after his Christmas break! Dr John Ross of the local Naval Hospital had volunteered to monitor Randy's sleep on subsequent nights and at 6 am Randy fell asleep. He had achieved his world record of 264 hours without sleep and it is reported that it took him a mere three seconds to fall asleep after his head hit the pillow. He slept for 14 hours and 40 minutes, and felt well enough to go to school the next day. The following night he slept for ten and a half hours before being woken to go to school. It was estimated that Randy had missed out on approximately 75 hours sleep over the 11-day period. He did not fully make up for this lost sleep in subsequent nights, although he did experience 'REM rebound' and recovered most of this sleep stage. In all, only 24 per cent of his total sleep loss was recovered. This evidence suggests that REM sleep is a particularly important type of sleep. In contrast to his earlier conclusions based on the Tripp study, the Randy Gardner case led Dement to conclude that sleep deprivation does *not* inevitably lead to psychosis. The loss of sleep did not make Randy 'crazy'. Some 40 years later, no psychologist has attempted to break Randy's record and it is unlikely that they will due to the possible dangers involved. Indeed, Dement questions whether any such proposed study would pass a university ethics committee today.

There have been other reports of human volunteers who have stayed awake for eight to ten days in carefully monitored laboratory situations. Like Randy, none of them has suffered serious physiological or psychological problems. Again like Randy, all of them suffered a gradual decline in concentration, motivation and perception as their sleep debt increased. All these volunteers recovered fully after a few nights' sleep.

It is often reported that Randy suffered no ill effects as a result of his marathon wake-athon. Indeed, Coren[4] states that, 'this conclusion is so widespread that it has now become a stock "fact" presented in virtually any psychology or psychiatry book that has a chapter on sleep'. However, Dement does mention some side-effects experienced by Randy. He notes that Randy's analytical abilities, memory, perception, motivation and motor control were all affected to varying degrees. He had delayed reactions and sometimes couldn't perform simple mathematical calculations. Nevertheless, many of these deficits are often not given the prominence that might have been expected.

John Ross of the US Navy Medical Neuropsychiatric Research Unit reports Gardner's symptoms in greater detail.[5] He reports that by day two, Randy had difficulty focusing his eyes and, by day four, he was suffering from hallucinations (he saw a street sign as a real person) and delusions (he thought he was a famous black football player), which continued on and off throughout the period of study. He had episodes of disjointed thinking and his attention span was extremely short. When asked to subtract backwards from 100 in blocks of seven, he could only reach 65 before forgetting the task. Coren remains convinced that 'prolonged sleep deprivation does lead to the appearance of serious mental symptoms'. Equally, Dement[6] retorts that 'I can say with absolute certainty that staying awake for 264 hours did not cause any psychiatric problems whatsoever.'

It is generally accepted that Randy showed some definite neurological changes. The dispute centres on the *extent* of his symptoms. Were his symptoms relatively minor or more serious? The former view suggests that sleep deprivation doesn't cause mental health problems; the latter suggests the opposite. Dement proposed that Randy coped well with a lack of sleep because he was young and physically fit. It has subsequently been demonstrated in animal studies that such factors are vitally important in how rats cope with sleep deprivation.

So did Randy provide us with the answer to the question of whether sleep is necessary for normal human functioning? As already mentioned, researchers continue to dispute the Randy Gardner case and it is also worth pointing out that there are a number of problems with sleep-deprivation studies. Perhaps the most important concerns the argument that an understanding of sleep deprivation does not logically imply the function of sleep. For example, other physiological mechanisms might compensate for any effects of the loss of sleep. This has been shown to occur in molecular biology, where the knockout of a particular gene does not always lead to a clear phenotype. Conversely, a behaviour that is adversely affected by sleep loss, although it suggests that sleep plays a role in that behaviour, does not prove that sleep alone is responsible for it. In addition, since the Gardner study, researchers have demonstrated the existence of momentary lapses into sleep, called 'microsleeps'. These last for only a few seconds but Dement accepts that Randy probably experienced these. They are only evident with continuous physiological recording equipment, so any future study would need to employ such techniques to ensure that these 'microsleeps' don't add up to a significant amount of sleep over a long period.

William Dement, as one of the world's leading experts on sleep, was involved in both the Peter Tripp and Randy Gardner cases. He reports conflicting results from each and explains the reasons for his conclusions from each. Despite arguing that Randy Gardner suffered few side-effects from his sleep-deprivation marathon, Dement believes that a lack of sleep *can* have severe consequences. He argues that major industrial disasters such as the grounding of the *Exxon Valdez*, the crash of the space shuttle *Challenger* and the nuclear disaster at Chernobyl can all be traced back to decisions made by people who were suffering from lack of sleep. He estimates that 24,000 car fatalities in the USA each year are also attributable to tiredness. He suggests that the average adult needs about eight hours of sleep per night and recommends that people do not build up a sleep debt.

Randy Gardner subsequently got a job with one of the sleep researchers after successfully completing his education. He suffered no long-term effects as a result of his sleep-deprivation exploits, and is now retired and still living in San Diego. Randy will for ever be known in the scientific literature as 'the boy who didn't sleep'.

1. Jouvet, M. (1967) Mechanisms of the states of sleep: a neuropharmacological approach. *Research Publications: Association for Research in Nervous and Mental Diseases* 45, pp. 86–126.
2. Patrick, G.T. and Gilbert, J.A. (1896) On the effects of loss of sleep. *Psychology Review* 3, pp. 469–83.
3. According to Pinel, J. (2000) *Biopsychology*. Boston: Allyn & Bacon, the record for time spent awake is attributed to Mrs Maureen Weston (449 hours, or 18 days, 17 hours) (p. 322). The *Guinness Book of World Records* (1990), however, attributes the record to Robert McDonald, who spent 453 hours, 40 minutes awake in a rocking chair. Different attempts are assessed in different ways and this is reflected in the different 'records'.
4. Coren, S. (1998) Sleep deprivation, psychosis and mental efficiency. *Psychiatric Times* XV(3), March.
5. Ross, J.J. (1965) Neurological findings after prolonged sleep deprivation. *Archives of Neurology* 12, pp. 399–403.
6. Dement, W. and Vaughan, C. (2001) *The Promise of Sleep*. London: Pan Books.

9 The 'twins' case: David Reimer, the boy who was never a girl

Bruce Reimer was born on 22 August 1965, the elder of twin boys. Eight months later, while undergoing a routine circumcision, his penis was accidentally burnt off. After consulting world-renowned sex researcher Dr John Money of Johns Hopkins University in Baltimore, his parents decided it was in the best interests of Bruce to raise him as a girl, to be called Brenda. This involved a surgical sex change and a 12-year programme of social and mental readjustment. The case was reported in the scientific literature as an unqualified success and, unbeknown to Bruce, he became one of the most famous case studies in medical and psychological literature. The so-called 'twins' case allowed for a greater exploration of gender identity and the classic nature versus nurture argument. Infant sex reassignments, where a child is born with ambiguous genitalia, continue to this day, based in part on evidence from this case. In reality, however, the experiment had been a total failure. On being told of his past, 'Brenda' chose to resume his life as a man, David Reimer, and until recently, he lived with his wife and family in Winnipeg, Canada.[1] In 2004, however, his life took another tragic turn. Having lost his job and separated from his wife, as well as mourning the death of his twin brother, Reimer committed suicide on 4 May. He was 38.

Background

Ron and Janet Reimer grew up with similar rural backgrounds near Winnipeg, Canada. They were both descended from families of Mennonites, a strict religious sect rather similar to the Amish. Both teenagers felt restricted by their religions and in their late teens went to live in the city. Janet got a job as a waitress, Ron in a slaughterhouse – honest jobs for honest, hard-working people. They married on 19 December 1964 and dreamt of having twins. Just a few months later, the dream came true. They named their twin boys Bruce and Brian. Although they were identical twins, Janet and Ron could distinguish between them and they found that Bruce was by far the more active child. The family looked forward to a contented, simple and happy life.

When the twins were about seven months old, Janet noticed that they seemed to be distressed while urinating. She took them to the doctor and they were diagnosed with a condition called phimosis, in which the foreskin is too tight. This is easily rectified by circumcision. Janet arranged for both circumcisions to take place on 27 April 1966. On the day of the operations, the usual doctor could not perform the surgery, so Dr Jean-Marie Huot, a general practitioner, stood in. A nurse was sent to collect one of the twins for the first operation and, purely by chance, she picked up Bruce.

Confusion surrounds the exact details of the operation, but it appears that an artery clamp was applied to Bruce's foreskin. Then rather than using a scalpel to remove the foreskin, Dr Huot used a Bovie cautery machine. This employs an electric current, allied to a sharp cutting device, to burn the edges of the incision and thus seal the blood vessels to prevent bleeding. It was unnecessary, however, to use both a clamp and the cautery machine – and indeed dangerous, since the clamp could have conducted the electric current on to the penis. When the machine's needle failed to cut successfully the first time, the current was increased. This time, the effects were devastating: Bruce's penis was burned right down to its base. He was fitted with a catheter and Brian's operation was cancelled.

Within two weeks of the operation, the bits of Bruce's burnt penis had dried up and flaked off until nothing was left. There was no possibility of restoring the organ to its original state. Ron and Janet were told by their local hospital that the best course of action was for Bruce to have an artificial phallus fitted prior to him starting school. Phalloplasty was in its infancy in the 1960s, so they were informed by an eminent psychiatrist that in the future Bruce would have to realise that 'he is incomplete, physically defective and that he must live apart'.

Ron and Janet returned home with the twins in a state of shock. Adding to their distress was the realisation that Brian's phimosis had cleared up on its own accord – Bruce had not even needed the circumcision in the first place. The botched operation had a devastating effect on the family. Ron told a couple of close friends at work about the operation but they had joked about it, so Ron and Janet made the decision to try to keep details of the operation secret. They believed this would protect the family from ill-meaning gossip, but it also had the effect of isolating them. They became prisoners in their own home since they didn't want to risk any childminder finding out the truth if he or she was required to change Bruce's nappy.

A possible solution?

Ten months after the operation, Ron and Janet sat down to watch a current affairs programme, little knowing that what they were about to watch would be the catalyst for an even worse chain of events. On the programme that night was Dr John Money from Johns Hopkins University in Baltimore. Money was one of the world's leading sex researchers, and a charismatic and persuasive academic. On the show, he announced that his team was successfully conducting transsexual surgery. He argued that it was possible for an individual to change gender successfully. He claimed that assigned sex was the best indicator of an individual's future gender and a transsexual appeared on-screen and stated that she was now far happier and more accepted in society as a woman. The programme moved to the topic of intersex children (children born with ambiguous genitalia). Money explained that, through surgery, socialisation and hormone replacement, children could be raised successfully in whatever sex was assigned to them. He stated that genetic sex does not have to correspond with psychological sex (gender).[2,3] Ron and Janet were mesmerised by Dr Money; they wrote to him straight away, giving details of their situation. Money, realising the unique nature of the case, wrote by return of post.

He knew that their case was important: he had long argued that an intersex child's gender identity was not determined at birth and proposed the theory of 'gender neutrality'. He believed that in intersex cases surgeons should 'assign' the most appropriate gender at birth because such children were 'gender neutral' at birth. Critics argued that this theory could apply only to a small sub-group of the population, namely children born with ambiguous genitalia, or hermaphrodites. Money, however, believed that his theory of gender neutrality could be applied to *all* children and that Bruce provided him with a unique opportunity to prove his theory, especially as his identical twin, Brian, would be a perfectly matched control. If a normal male child could successfully be reared as a girl, it would surely show that sexuality is, indeed, undifferentiated at birth in *all* children. It would help make a major contribution to the long-running nature–nurture debate in psychology: are we what we are because of our genetic inheritance or are we what we are because of our upbringing and environmental experiences after birth? If Money could resolve this debate in terms of sexuality, he would become one of the world's most famous and respected academics. He couldn't believe his good fortune, it was too good an opportunity to miss.

Money immediately invited the Reimer family to Johns Hopkins University to discuss the case. At about the same time, a young graduate called Milton Diamond started his postgraduate career examining the effects of hormones on human behaviour. Diamond was working at the University of Kansas and was unconvinced by Money's theory of neutrality. Indeed, he believed that gender-specific behaviour was pre-programmed in the womb. The Kansas team tested this by creating hermaphrodite guinea pigs; they did this by injecting pregnant females with testosterone. The resultant female guinea pigs were born with clitorises the size of penises. The key question was whether these female guinea pigs would demonstrate male or female behaviour. The answer was that the testosterone-treated females acted like males by attempting to mount unaffected females. The team members believed that they had shown that pre-birth experiences determine subsequent gender-specific behaviour. In other words, in guinea pigs at least, masculine behaviour could be programmed before birth, regardless of their actual sex. This seemed directly to contradict the theory of gender neutrality at birth, but the findings had been tested only on animals, so it was unclear whether they were applicable to human behaviour.

Diamond, however, was adamant that Money was wrong. He argued that pre-birth factors were of overriding importance for gender identity, and that socialisation plays a subsidiary role. Diamond believed that while it might be true that hermaphrodites could be steered successfully into either gender, the theory of gender neutrality could not apply to all 'normal' newborns. Diamond even threw down the gauntlet to Money, suggesting that to support his theory he would have to provide an instance of a normal male successfully raised as a female. The 'twins case' meant that Money could do just that, and Diamond's views would be largely ignored for years to come.

From boy to girl?

When the Reimers first met John Money they immediately felt that he was someone they could work with. Janet and Ron regarded him as a 'god' and were happy to place their complete trust in him. Money explained that Bruce could be raised successfully as a girl and develop successfully as a woman. He would be able to have sexual intercourse as a woman and would be attracted to men. Ron and Janet were unaware that Money was recommending a course of action that had never been attempted before with a child born as a fully functioning male. Money was impatient for the go-ahead from Ron and Janet since he believed that the gender reassignment had to take place prior to the child's second birthday. After considerable deliberation, Ron and Janet came to their decision. They believed it would be easier for Bruce to be raised as one of the 'gentler' sex and that the problems he would have suffered as a man without a penis would have been too hard to bear. On 3 July 1967, Bruce was surgically castrated and, choosing a name with the same initial, his parents renamed him Brenda. The Reimers returned home with strict instructions from Money about how to bring up their daughter and they slavishly followed his advice from that moment on. They immediately let Brenda's hair grow, dolls were bought and no mention was ever made of the tragedy that had occurred. To all intents and purposes, the Reimers had two non-identical twins: a boy and a girl.

Looking at the twins, strangers saw two beautiful, non-identical children. Brian with his short brown hair and Brenda with her shoulder-length wavy hair. However, this difference disappeared as soon as Brenda moved or spoke. In everything Brenda did she was masculine. She would never play with the toys she had been given as a girl, she would always borrow Brian's. She would play physical games, want toy guns, play soldiers and use a toy carpentry set that Brian had been given. Brian later reported that she would walk like a boy, sit with her legs apart and usually win any fights that the twins had. Indeed, Brenda was described as the 'male' leader of the pair. For Brenda, this was confusing, and it was also somewhat upsetting for Brian. Moncy dismissed all these facets of Brenda's behaviour as 'tomboyism' and continued to insist that Ron and Janet bring Brenda up as a girl.

There were other more obvious clues as to Brenda's past. Brenda would insist on standing up facing the toilet when urinating. Her kindergarten teacher noted that she was 'more of a boy than a girl' and, of course, her fellow students also noticed such differences. Brenda started to have behavioural and emotional problems at school. Despite her delicate looks (Janet always dressed her in the most feminine of clothes) she would often end up fighting with the boys and come home covered in mud. Brenda had been given an IQ test by Money and had scored 90, placing her slightly below average intelligence, but her performance at school was much worse. Ron and Janet had never told the school of Brenda's troubled history, but to avoid her being placed one year behind her peer group they finally informed her teachers.

The struggle Brenda was experiencing at school was in marked contrast to the academic success that John Moncy was now enjoying. Since the 1950s, Money had argued that post-birth environmental factors were of overriding importance for gender identity. He had cited evidence on intersex twins who had been brought up successfully as different genders and now he produced the 'twins' case to support his argument. Here, Money had two identical boys whose experiences pre-birth followed the normal male pattern, and one was now living successfully as a girl. Money made no mention of Brenda's problems beyond the comment that she did express some tomboyish traits as a result of copying her brother. To Money's eager audiences around the world, the argument was over: the ultimate experiment had shown that boys and girls are made, not born.

The 'twins' case was an immediate sensation. Scientific textbooks were rewritten, saying evidence now showed that nurture was of overriding importance in gender identity. At this time in psychology, behaviourism was the pre-eminent paradigm and Money's ideas seemed to fit well with this approach. The Women's Rights movement took up the argument, suggesting that biological differences no longer explained gender differences. Surgeons and parents who had for years wondered what to do when faced with an intersex child more readily agreed to immediate genital surgery. After all, if a male child could be brought up successfully as a girl, an intersex child should have even fewer problems. The ramifications of the 'twins' case were far-reaching and Money basked in them all.

There was at least one dissenting voice, though. Diamond was still not convinced by the gender neutrality argument. He argued that the 'twins' case merely highlighted the wonderful adaptability of human behaviour, but that biology still played a central part in sexual identity. Diamond could not believe that biology did not play a key role and, indeed, there had by now been some cases where male children born with micro-penises had been surgically reassigned as girls only to revert back to being male at adolescence. In addition, methodological problems with Money's research were highlighted. A paper outlining these was almost prevented from being published due to Money's insistence and far-reaching influence. When these concerns were published they were virtually ignored. Money was a world-famous academic and the 'twins' case was regarded as the final conclusive proof of his theory of gender neutrality. Money advocated sex-reassignment surgery at birth for children born with ambiguous genitalia and this procedure was adopted in every major country in the world, with the exception of China. It is clear now that the 'twins' case should serve as a reminder of the dangers of blindly accepting an expert's view, and particularly the view of one who is considered pre-eminent in their field.

Research doubts?

As part of Brenda's reassignment, the family made annual visits to Johns Hopkins University in Baltimore to see John Money. Each time, Brenda reacted with horror and fear. From the age of four, she fought, hit and kicked anyone who tried to perform any test on her. Brian was also required to accompany Brenda and he too found the visits extremely upsetting. Gradually, it dawned on the twins that something was amiss. Why did they have to undertake such visits – visits that none of their friends undertook? Brenda could not understand why most of the questions focused on sex and gender. On being asked to undertake the standard 'draw a person' test that is supposed to help identify a child's gender identity, she drew a stick figure of a boy. When asked whom she had drawn, she simply answered 'Me.' Gradually, Brenda and Brian began to realise what answers were required of them. The term 'demand characteristics' refers to a situation where a participant guesses the purpose of a study and adjusts his or her behaviour accordingly. This is exactly what the twins began to do, thus results reported by Money may have been contaminated by this bias. Of course, Money was aware of such methodological problems and tried to probe the twins' answers, but it must have been increasingly difficult for him to remain objective as he began to obtain the answers he was hoping for.

One incident stands out in this respect. Money asked Brenda about a trip to a local zoo. He asked her which type of animal she would like to be if she could be changed into one. Brenda suggested a monkey. When Money asked her whether she would prefer to be a boy monkey or a girl monkey, he reports that she replied 'a girl'. This was taken by Money as evidence of Brenda's gender preference. However, years later David Reimer (Brenda) argued that he had said 'a gorilla' in answer to the question. Ignoring any deliberate misreporting by Money, this can be taken as evidence of a researcher hearing the answers he wanted to hear.

In adulthood, the twins reported that Money had presented himself in very different ways during these sessions. When Ron and Janet were present, he presented an image of the 'friendly uncle', but when they were absent he could be quite threatening towards them. It is reported that he asked the six-year-old twins to perform simulated sex with one another. On other occasions, he showed them sexually explicit pictures to try to reinforce their gender identities. Indeed, Money has written that such pictures can form a useful part of a child's sex education. Ron and Janet were entirely unaware of all such instances. They had to offer bribes to the twins, such as trips to Disneyland, to get them to continue the visits.

When Brenda was seven years of age, Money started to talk about the possibility of her having further vaginal surgery. He argued that many of Brenda's problems occurred because she was aware that she was different to other girls. Brenda was indeed aware of this and could not apparently even bring herself to look between her legs. Money enlisted the help of Ron and Janet to keep up with their 'homework assignments'. These involved talking to Brenda about her genitalia and the surgery. Brenda was particularly upset since she felt that her parents were now working with John Money and against her wishes. Nevertheless, Brenda remained adamant that she would not agree to any surgery. Under extreme pressure from Money and constantly unhappy at school, she eventually had a nervous breakdown.

Family doubts?

At around this time, Ron and Janet were beginning to have doubts about their original decision. They could see how unhappy Brenda was and were aware that the reassignment did not appear to be working. However, they trusted John Money, they had put their faith in him and they could see very little option but to continue with the path set out for them. Their situation was intolerable. Brian was also having behavioural difficulties. He was jealous of all the attention Brenda got and was caught shoplifting at a local store. In desperation and in need of a new start, the Reimers sold their house and moved west to British Columbia. Rather than giving them a fresh start, though, the move was a disaster. Brenda became even more isolated at school, Ron became engrossed in his work at a sawmill and hit the bottle on returning home each day, and Janet became prone to bouts of serious depression. On one occasion, she swallowed a bottle full of sleeping pills but was saved by Ron's timely intervention. The family eventually decided to return to Winnipeg. Brenda believed that many of the family problems were directly attributable to her and vowed to try to save her parent's marriage by becoming more feminine. Unfortunately, her efforts were hampered by various physiological changes that emphasised her masculinity. These included a deepening of her voice and the development of a more male musculature and masculine facial features.

Brenda continued to have problems at school. She was shunned as a misfit, but managed to join a group of tomboys and develop some tentative friendships. Other classmates ridiculed her and called her 'cavewoman'. She was eventually banned from using the girls' toilet when she was caught urinating standing up. She had to sneak out to a quiet side street to go to the toilet. Not surprisingly, Brenda became increasingly troubled. Local psychiatrists were assigned to her case and became perplexed in trying to reconcile the reality of Brenda with the academic reports of her written by John Money that they had read. Nevertheless, not one of them questioned the original decision to rear her as a girl. They realised that it was now too late to do anything else. They needed to persuade Brenda to take oestrogen, the female hormone, to facilitate the effects of female puberty. Brenda resolutely refused to take any such medication. The last thing she wanted was to become more feminine. However, after constant badgering, and with little choice, Brenda agreed to take the medication in a last ditch attempt to fit in. This was around the time of her 12th birthday. Even so, whenever the opportunity arose, she flushed the pills down the toilet. She also began bouts of binge eating, thinking in her desperation that an increase in her weight would disguise the effects of the oestrogen.

The local psychiatrists discussed Brenda's case. She had reported that she knew she was physiologically different from 'normal' children and that she had been told by her father of 'some mistake'. On further questioning, Brenda said that she thought her mother might have beaten her between the legs. This statement appeared to fit in well with Freud's theory of psychosexual development, where he hypothesised that boys have a sexual desire for their mothers. He called this the Oedipus complex, after the Greek tragedy in which a young man unknowingly slays his father and then marries his mother. Freud's theory held that a boy realises he is in competition with his father for his mother's affection. When he realises that his father is far more powerful than him, he begins to suffer from 'castration anxiety' – that is, the worry that his father will emasculate him. To avoid this, but still to impress his mother, he then adopts the behaviour of his father. That, then, is why boys turn out like their fathers. Freud argued that girls, on the other hand, experience the Electra complex: when a girl realises that she lacks a penis she suffers from 'penis envy' and places the blame for this absence on her mother. What Brenda had done could indeed be interpreted in exactly this way: she placed the blame for her lack of a penis on her mother. In order to try to possess a penis, girls choose their fathers as their primary love object (symbolically, a girl, in having sexual relations with her father, may repossess the penis). According to psychoanalytic therapy, it is beneficial to recognise and try to resolve many of these issues.

Of course, one of the problems with psychoanalytic theory is that any number of other possible interpretations can be placed on the situation. When Janet was told that Brenda wondered whether she had abused her, she was horrified. Something had to be done. Janet asked Brenda whether there was any point in continuing with their annual visits to see Money. When Brenda said no, their trip was cancelled, and, to the relief of everyone in the family, they never visited Baltimore again.

What was my name?

In 1979, the BBC sent an investigative team to Winnipeg and Baltimore to investigate the 'twins' case as part of a film on gender identity. They contacted Brenda's psychiatrists and also spoke to Money. Although Money initially welcomed their interest the reporters mentioned that they had spoken to other academics who were questioning the success of the case. The main critic cited was once again Milton Diamond. On being told this, Money immediately threw out the BBC reporters and wrote a threatening letter to the Director General of the BBC, warning of legal action and compensation claims for any harm caused to the Reimers. Ignoring this, the BBC programme was aired, but did not have the impact expected among the academic community. Despite obvious criticisms, Money's reputation remained intact and his evidence on the 'twins' case unquestioned. With no further access to Brenda, Money's direct public pronouncements on the case ceased after 1980. Money explained his reluctance to publish any follow-up on the case as being due to the inappropriate intrusion of the media.

The months rolled by with Brenda increasingly displaying a boy's persona. She became more and more boyish in her words, dress and actions. Brenda's local psychiatric team believed that the time was right for Brenda to be told the truth about her birth. The Reimers agreed. One day, Ron picked up Brenda from the local psychologist and offered to buy her an ice cream. Brenda feared the worst, since bad news often accompanied a trip to get an ice cream. Ron started telling Brenda of her birth and the accident that had followed. While Ron cried, Brenda remained dry-eyed, staring straight ahead. She experienced a myriad of different emotions: disbelief, incredulity and anger, but most of all relief. At last there was an explanation, however horrific, for all the difficulties she had faced. Brenda asked only one question of her father: 'What was my name?'

Immediately, Brenda decided to revert to her biological sex. The main problem was deciding how this was to be done. After all, it's not something that can be changed as simply as one changes clothes. Such a decision was bound to attract unwelcome comment and Brenda was well aware of the hurt that gossip and innuendo can cause. She did not want to revert to her former name, Bruce, as she didn't like it. Eventually she chose David, after King David, since the name was associated with overcoming difficulties of Goliath-like proportions. One week after his 15th birthday, David made his first public outing at a family wedding. He began to have testosterone injections instead of the oestrogen he had been taking and underwent a painful double mastectomy. Just before his 16th birthday he had further surgery to construct an artificial penis.

The twins concocted a story that Brenda had died in a plane crash and said that David was Brian's long-lost cousin. It seemed to convince some people, and there were others that didn't want to ask exactly what was happening. Although David was far happier as a boy, there were still painful experiences ahead for him. He couldn't stop thinking about the doctor who had performed the botched circumcision and decided to seek his revenge. He bought a second-hand gun and found out the doctor's name and current place of work. He went to the hospital where Dr Huot was working and found his room. David entered the room with the gun in his pocket. Referring to the botched operation, David asked him whether he realised the hell he had put him through. This alerted

Dr Huot to the intruder's identity and he started to cry. At this, David left. He went to a nearby river, threw the gun in and he too began to cry.

Becoming a man

When David turned 18, he became legally entitled to a sum of money ($170,000) he had been awarded in an out-of-court claim settled by St Boniface Hospital 16 years earlier (this was the hospital where his botched operation had taken place – his parents had sued it for damages, although the 'facts' of what had happened were never 'officially' agreed). With a small proportion of this money, David bought a van, which was (ironically) known to him and his friends by the nick-name 'The Shaggin' Wagon'. In fact, when out with girlfriends, David always made excuses that allowed him to refrain from actually having sex with them, and often pretended to pass out from the effects of imbibing too much alcohol. On one occasion, he *actually* did pass out and in the morning it was obvious that his girlfriend had discovered his secret. Unfortunately, having been told his full life history, she couldn't stop herself from telling others and, once again, David was the object of gossip, ridicule and innuendo. He was later discovered uncon-scious by his parents, having taken an overdose, and Janet remembers asking Ron if they ought to leave him to die in peace, having suffered enough. Without wait-ing for Ron to answer, however, Janet rushed him to the local hospital to have his stomach pumped. During his recovery, David withdrew into himself and spent long periods isolated in a log cabin in a forest near Lake Winnipeg.

The final tragedy

Near his 22nd birthday, David had another phalloplasty and was delighted with the results. Brian's wife knew a young woman called Jane who had three children but was now a single parent. A blind date was arranged between Jane and David. The two of them were friends from the moment they met. Jane had already been told of David's troubled history and it seemingly made no difference to her feel-ings for him. On 22 September 1990, David and Jane were married and got on with their family life. At this time, David was described as possessing a keen sense of humour, he was said to be a self-assured man who enjoyed both his work and his young family. He was quoted as having accepted his past but not forgotten it. He was at last settled and able to enjoy a normal family life, one that included sexual intercourse with his wife.

David particularly resented his surgical castration, which had ensured that he was unable to have children of his own. Up until 1990, David was never actually aware of how famous he was as an academically cited case study. He certainly never believed that people thought his case had been a success. On discovering the truth, David dropped his anonymity to try to publicise the circumstances of his case. He wanted to act as a warning to others who found themselves in similar situations. He went public with his story, even appearing on the *Oprah Winfrey Show*. In 2000, David even wrote to John Money asking for a meeting and an apology from him. In spite of his own combative nature, Money refused to meet him.

Unfortunately, tragedy was to strike the Reimer family yet again. In 2002 Brian, who had been suffering from schizophrenia, died. He had passed away alone in his flat and his body had lain undiscovered for three days. Although it was suspected that suicide may have been the cause of his death, Janet Reimer insisted that the real cause was a brain haemorrhage. Losing his identical twin in such circumstances had a profound effect on David. He withdrew into his grief, visiting his brother's grave virtually every day, and suffered long bouts of depression. Despite a history of mental illness in the family, David seemed to blame himself for his brother's death. Brian had always received less attention than him and, of course, had also been lied to by his parents regarding the exact circumstances of his brother's birth. He, too, had been traumatised by the annual visits to see John Money, and had been teased by workmates when David went public with his story. Irrationally, David blamed himself for all this. Continuing his downward spiral, David lost his job and separated from his wife Jane and, in turn, lost the close contact he had once enjoyed with his stepchildren, who had started to call him 'Dad'. Thanks to a disastrous business decision, David had also lost $35,000 that he had received from a film production company as part of a deal to make a film about his life. Given such circumstances, and taking into account his life history, it was perhaps no great surprise that, on 4 May 2004, David Reimer committed suicide. He drove to a local supermarket car park and shot himself with a sawn-off shotgun.

Janet Reimer laid the blame for both her sons' deaths on the unusual circumstances of their upbringing. A spokesman for Johns Hopkins University issued a statement on behalf of John Money, reiterating his policy not to comment on the 'twins' case.

Research fall-out

Although John Money made no direct reference to the 'twins' case after 1980, he continued to promote the theory of gender neutrality and the success of gender reassignment surgery. This continued despite the fact that a researcher in California had shown that testosterone injections could increase penis size in children born with micro-penises. In the early 1990s, a determined Milton Diamond set out to discover the truth about the 'twins' case. Rumours abounded that all was not as reported by Money, yet it remained the most influential piece of research into gender identity.

With the help of the BBC, Diamond eventually tracked down David and (with David's consent) wrote a paper[4] presenting evidence that David had not accepted the sex role in which he was reared. An indication of Money's continuing pervasive influence is demonstrated by the fact that it took two years for Diamond to secure publication for this explosive paper; many people were upset by and disbelieving of its findings and conclusions. In the paper, Diamond appeared effectively to demolish many of the arguments put forward by Money. He argued that individuals are *not* psychosexually neutral at birth and that psychosexual development is not determined by genitalia or upbringing – that is to say, you cannot change a child's genitalia and upbringing and expect them to adopt the chosen gender successfully. As David himself put it, 'If a woman lost her breasts would you turn her into a guy?'

Diamond cites other studies that suggest a neurological basis for sexual behaviour.[5, 6] It is suggested here that the most important organ in determining gender identity is actually the brain, not the genitals. Indeed, there have been other case studies which have reported that boys with micro-penises never doubt their correct assignment as males[7] and the case of a girl who, after declaring herself to be a boy at 14, subsequently found herself to be chromosomally male.[8] An increasingly influential group called the Intersex Society of North America (ISNA), comprising 400 intersex individuals, also advocates the abandonment of genital reassignment surgery for infants. Such individuals continue to call for this change despite the fact that it causes them additional distress as they are implicitly criticising parental decisions taken many years before.

Diamond concludes that there is no known case where a chromosomal male has 'easily and fully accepted an imposed life as a female regardless of physical and medical intervention'. He suggests that chromosomally normal males should be raised as males and that surgical intervention should conform to this decision despite the greater difficulties with this type of surgery. Immediate surgery and sex reassignment as a female may *appear* a more favourable, and easier, immediate solution but is unlikely to be so in the long term. Despite such arguments, many of Money's ideas are still followed and sex reassignment at birth continues to this day.

Subsequently, Money published an article detailing reasons why David's case should not be taken as evidence for the failure of the gender neutrality theory. Despite at one time arguing that David provided the classic test for his theory, Money argued instead that the special circumstances of the case mean that little can be concluded from it. Initially, it was thought that if a child born male could be brought up successfully as a girl this would prove the case. Now Money argues that because David was born a normal male his case can have no bearing on the thousands of intersex children born each year.

It is estimated that sex reassignment surgery for intersex cases accounts for about 1000 operations per year worldwide. Diamond questions these procedures and declares that the evidence is not there to support this course of action. He suggests a conservative approach, whereby gender assignment should be guided by the sex chromosomes of an individual, and believes that surgery should be delayed until the gender preference of the child is clear. Infants should still be assigned a gender at birth, but no surgery should be performed until a clear gender identity is established. Money, on the other hand, argues that a child cannot remain an 'it' until its gender preference is clear, and that gender reassignment at birth is preferable.

Indeed, many parents still favour gender reassignment and give permission for surgical procedures to commence soon after birth. They tend to feel that they would be placing an intolerable burden on their child by leaving them with ambiguous genitalia. Money echoes this by arguing that to follow Diamond's advice would be to wreck the lives of unknown numbers of intersex children by causing them profound psychological harm during their early years.

However, the tide appears to be turning in favour of the more conservative treatment of intersex children, and there is little doubt that had his accident occurred today Bruce would have been brought up a boy. Nevertheless, while academics continue to debate the best course of action, the short life of David Reimer, 'the ultimate case study', serves as a poignant reminder of the crucial importance of their discussions.

1. Much of this chapter is based on a fascinating book on this case, written with David Reimer's consent: John Calapinto (2000) *As Nature Made Him: The Boy who was Raised a Girl.* New York: HarperCollins.
2. Although the terms 'sex' and 'gender' are often used interchangeably in the literature, here sex will refer to biological or genetic sex, whereas gender will refer to the sex a person feels him/herself to be.
3. Diamond, M. and Sigmundson, H.K. (1997) Sex reassignment at birth: a long term review and clinical implications. *Archives of Pediatric & Adolescent Medicine* 151, pp. 298–304.
4. Diamond and Sigmundson, Sex reassignment at birth.
5. Le Vay, S. (1991) A difference in the hypothalamic structure between heterosexual and homosexual men. *Science* 253, pp. 1034–7.

6. Swaab, D.F. and Fliers, E. (1985) A sexually dimorphic nucleus in the human brain. *Science* 228, pp. 1112–5.
7. Reilly, J.M. and Woodhouse, C.R. (1989) Small penis and the male sexual role. *Journal of Urology* 142, pp. 569–72.
8. Reiner, W.G. (1996) Case study: sex reassignment in a teenage girl. *Journal of the American Academy of Child and Adolescent Psychiatry* 35, pp. 799–803.

10 The man who lived with a hole in his head: the story of Phineas Gage

Phineas Gage was a railway foreman working in the 1840s near Vermont. He was responsible for blasting rock in order to prepare the way for the laying of railway tracks. One day he made a disastrous mistake and his one-metre tamping iron, used to pack down the explosive powder blasts, shot off and landed 30 feet away. Unfortunately, on its way it entered Gage's chin and exited through the top of his head. Amazingly, he lived to tell the tale, but with a changed personality as a result of his accident. He became a textbook case in brain science and was known as 'the man who lived with a hole in his head'.

The luckiest man alive

On 13 September 1848, Phineas Gage[1, 2] went to work as usual, little knowing that by the end of the day he would be the luckiest man alive. His job was to organise a gang of workers to clear a path through granite rock ready for the construction of a new railway line. He was an exceptionally good worker, very thorough and meticulous, and popular with his colleagues. He took charge of laying the explosives personally. This was a dangerous job but one that suited Phineas's precise personality. The procedure for laying explosives was always the same: his assistant would place the powder in a hole drilled in the rock; Phineas would then carefully press down the powder before his assistant set the fuse and filled the hole with sand; finally, Phineas would use his metre-long iron rod to tamp down the sand to act as a plug so that the blast would channel down into the rock. Phineas was an acknowledged expert with the tamping rod. Indeed, he had had his own custom-made by the local blacksmith. No one is certain exactly whose fault it was, but Phineas began tamping down the powder before his assistant had added the sand. It seems most likely that a spark caused by the iron rod hitting the granite had set off the explosive, and this sent the tamping iron flying into the air with Phineas still leaning over it.

The iron rod landed about 30 feet away, covered with blood and bits of Phineas's brain. The rod had entered his head under his left cheekbone, passed through his mouth and exited a fraction of a second later from the middle of his forehead, just above his hairline. His workmates ran up to him, assuming he was dead. Unbelievably, Phineas sat up with blood pouring from the exit wound. He was conscious and coherent, and immediately started talking about the incident. He was placed on an oxcart and taken to the nearest town, less than a mile away, for treatment by the local doctor. When Dr Harlow turned up half an hour later, Phineas even joked about the extent of his injuries while sitting on the porch of the hotel he had been taken to. Although in considerable pain, Phineas was helped by the fact that there are no pain receptors in the brain, only on the outside surface of the skull.

Phineas's injuries and a conflict of views

Dr Harlow couldn't believe the extent of Phineas's injuries. There was little his medical expertise could do to help in such a situation, so he simply shaved Phineas's head, removed some bone and brain fragments, and pressed the larger pieces of skull that were still attached to it back into place. He cleaned the skin and bandaged the wound. He left the hole in Phineas's mouth untreated so that the wound could drain. There was little doubt, in the doctor's opinion, that Phineas would be dead in a few hours. The town cabinet maker came to measure Phineas in order to make a coffin ready for him. Over the first few days after his injury, however, Phineas did remarkably well, managing to stay alert and talkative. However, the wound soon began to give off a terrible smell because it had become infected and a fungus began to grow from Phineas's brain. In those days, there were disputes between doctors as to what should be done in such cases. Some believed that the fungus might be part of the regenerating brain and should be pushed back inside the cranium; others believed it should be removed. Dr Harlow let the fungus grow for a while, until a friend pointed out that surely one's recovery must be hampered by a fungus growing out of one's head! Frustrated by his lack of knowledge and appreciating the simple, but likely, truth of this remark, Dr Harlow immediately cut off the growth.

Phineas developed a fever and became delirious. Huge pockets of pus were drained from beneath his eyes. In those days, doctors knew nothing about bacterial infection, but the prognosis could not have been worse. Dr Harlow used the technique of 'bleeding' to draw off some of Phineas's blood (at that time, doctors believed, incorrectly, that patients suffered from having 'too much blood'). Luckily for Phineas this technique may indeed have helped him considerably, since it is possible that it reduced his blood pressure and thus helped to reduce the pressure on his swollen brain. The fact that his skull had a hole in it ensured that he had an 'open head' injury, which would also have allowed his swollen brain to expand within his cranium. Miraculously, 22 days after his accident, Phineas started to make a recovery and, within ten weeks, was pronounced fully recovered from his injuries. Admittedly, he had lost the sight in his left eye but apart from that he was physically restored to normal. However, although he had recovered physically, psychologically this was not the case.

'No longer Gage'

Dr Harlow reported that Phineas could perform all the tasks that he could prior to the accident, but somehow there was something strangely different about him. Dr Harlow worried about his mental state. Six months after the accident, Phineas returned to his former employers in order to reclaim his job. His physical capacities seemed restored, his speech was fine and his memory was intact. But although many reports suggest that Phineas had recovered all his physical powers there are conflicting accounts which state that there was evidence of continuing physical weakness. Far more marked than that, however, was the change evident in Phineas's personality: he was now unreliable, impatient, hostile, rude and abrupt; he used vulgar, coarse language, and changed his plans from one moment to the next. He had become disinhibited and a risk taker. He could not be trusted in such a state and was described by his doctor and his friends as 'no longer Gage'. No amount of persuasion or reasoning could make him change his ways; he seemed incapable of curtailing his offensive and unpredictable behaviour, even though it was obvious it was having a detrimental effect on his life. After a trial period Phineas's employers felt they had no option but to terminate his contract.

Meanwhile his case had started to attract the attention of other medical practitioners, particularly Dr Bigelow from Harvard University in Boston, Massachusetts. Bigelow arranged for Phineas to visit Harvard for a thorough examination of his case. In those days, there was no easy method for examining the brain; doctors were still trying to determine how it worked. One approach, of course, would be to examine unique cases such as that presented by Phineas, where a freak accident had led to specific damage to one area of the brain. At the time there were broadly two schools of thought regarding the workings of the brain. There were those such as Dr Bigelow who believed that the entire brain is involved in all thinking and behaviour, and that damage to one area of the brain would mean that other areas of the brain would compensate for this deficit.

The competing school of thought involved a belief in the so-called localisation of function of the brain (a view favoured by Dr Harlow). This suggested that specific areas of the brain have a specific function and that damage to one area would lead to a specific deficit in thinking or behaviour. The emerging 'science' of phrenology echoed this view and can still be seen demonstrated on replicated phrenological model heads. (Phrenology was a widely followed paradigm in the nineteenth century used to explain brain functioning. The functions of each region of the brain were determined by examining the external features of skulls. Bumps and indentations were related to the character of that person and, in such a way, a 'mental map' of the brain could be drawn up. Women in particular liked the idea of phrenology since no differences could be found between male and female skulls, thus it helped in their struggle to achieve equality with men.)

Followers of both schools of thought were particularly interested in cases such as that of Phineas Gage. It was rare indeed for doctors to be able to study the after-effects of such profound damage to a person's frontal lobes. In virtually all such cases, the injured person would undoubtedly have died from their injuries. As is often the way in such disputes, Gage's case was cited as evidence by both groups to support their views. On the one hand, it was argued that other areas of Phineas's brain must have taken over the function of the damaged areas, otherwise he would be either dead or much more profoundly affected than he actually was, and probably unable to think properly, control his movements, talk, and so forth. The Gage case was cited as supporting the idea that the brain is a complex, integrated organism working as one unit, and that it has an inbuilt flexibility that allows unaffected areas to take over destroyed areas. Dr Bigelow believed this view to be correct and may have deliberately underemphasised the character changes exhibited by Gage after the accident in order to strengthen his position.

Although conscious of the requirement to maintain patient confidentiality, Dr Harlow did report to trusted colleagues that Phineas was not his old self. This was taken as evidence that the areas of the brain destroyed were responsible for specific thoughts and behaviours that he now appeared to lack. These were primarily concerned with a lack of planning and reasoning, and a general disinhibition towards others demonstrated by his lack of respect and use of gross profanities. Purely by chance, the phrenological model included the regions of 'benevolence' (kindness) and 'agreeableness' in almost precisely the area that Phineas's rod had passed through. Thus, phrenologists and those who believed in the localisation of function in the brain also cited the Gage case as supporting *their* view. Because Harlow did not come forward publicly to report the character changes in Gage until many years after his death, Bigelow's reporting of the case held sway – namely that Gage remained virtually unaffected by the accident.

It is a fascinating aspect of the case that the same information can be used to provide evidence for competing schools of thought. However, looking back on the evidence with the benefit of today's increased knowledge, it is unsurprising that both groups used Gage to support their ideas since both were correct to some degree. We now know that the brain is an amazingly complex interconnected organism comprising 100 billion neurons, but that it does not work as a complete whole. It is perhaps more accurate to visualise individual circuits working together in the brain; with specific circuits operating specific functions. Even functions which do appear to be fairly localised to specific parts of the brain, such as face recognition or name recall, are interconnected to other areas. In essence, the brain can be viewed as *both* localised and interconnected. The one thing we *can* be certain of is that the 'science' of phrenology was incorrect.

'The only living man with a hole in his head'

Dr Bigelow declared the Gage case to be 'the most remarkable history of injury to the brain which has been recorded'. A plaster cast was made of his skull, which still resides in Harvard Medical School today. After a number of weeks spent exciting the interests of the medical school at Harvard, Phineas took to the road. There is some dispute as to what happened next in his life. It is possible that he travelled around the major towns in New England telling his story to paying customers who came to examine his skull and inspect his tamping iron. However, there are few records that can substantiate this. It has long been suggested that Phineas then took his tamping iron and trod the boards as a freak exhibit at P.T. Barnum's American Museum on Broadway. He is reported to have had a hole drilled in another skull so that he could show people the damage that had occurred to his own. He was billed as 'The only living man with a hole in the top of his head', and posters are said to have shown him with the iron bar still sticking out of his head! Although this is a great story, there is no collaborative evidence to support it and it seems likely that, if true, there would have been recorded evidence of his appearances from other sources. Indeed, it is unlikely that Phineas would have been much of a star attraction given that orang-utans, bearded ladies and 'mermaids' were also on display.

It appears that Phineas spent the next nine years in a series of jobs mainly concerned with horses. He first worked at a livery stables, and then it's most likely that he spent many years as a stagecoach driver working in Chile. In 1859, Phineas returned to live with his mother in San Francisco and took a variety of farm jobs. Each job turned out to be temporary, since he found it difficult to fit in and work with other people. Phineas started to have regular epileptic fits, of increasing frequency and magnitude. The doctors did not know the cause of these seizures, but it is likely that the head injuries he suffered from his accident played a part in them. Eventually, on 21 May 1860, Phineas Gage died.

He was buried without fuss in a small cemetery in San Francisco and no one would have heard any more of him except for the fact that, in 1866, Dr Harlow decided to try to find out what had happened to his most famous patient. Harlow managed to track down Phineas's mother who eventually agreed that Harlow could exhume Phineas's body and take his skull for donation to Harvard University Medical School. One other unusual item was also taken from Phineas's coffin: the tamping rod that blew the hole in his brain had been Phineas's constant companion in life and had accompanied him to his grave.

Armed with Phineas's skull and the tamping rod, and no longer concerned about patient confidentiality, Dr Harlow publicised the case of Phineas Gage. He argued that his injuries had changed his personality and that he had suffered a great deal from the diminishment of his social skills. Harlow could demonstrate that in the 11 years since his injury, Phineas's skull had not completely healed over and that he had lived, literally, with a hole in his head for all that time. Harlow can be credited with bringing the Gage case back to prominence and preventing him from being largely forgotten in the annals of medical history.

Further research

Similar skulls of people who have suffered injuries from arrows or from the effects of trepanning can be seen today in the Science Museum in London. Trepanning, or trephinning, is the most ancient form of brain surgery known. It involved boring a hole in the skull of a patient in the belief that this would help liberate bad spirits or demons. It can be considered among the earliest forms of psychosurgery. Trepanning may have been used for the alleviation of severe headaches due to intracranial pressure and, in such cases, may well have been a helpful therapy.

One year after Gage's death, a scientist called Paul Broca made a further breakthrough in our understanding of brain function thanks to a study of one of his patients, Leborgne, who had suffered a stroke. Leborgne could understand speech but was unable to produce it, with the exception of one word, 'tan' (the patient is often referred to as 'Tan' because of this). On Leborgne's death, it was discovered that he had particular damage to a small area of the brain in the lower part of the left frontal lobe. This was confirmed with other patient case studies and the region is now known as Broca's area. In 1874, Carl Wernicke found another area that is crucial for language comprehension. People who suffer from neurophysiological damage to this area (now known as Wernicke's area) are unable to understand the specific meaning or content of words while listen-ing, and unable to produce meaningful sentences; thus their speech has gram-matical structure but is without meaning. With these later insights, it seems amazing that Phineas did not suffer any speech or language deficits despite the nature of his injury.

Of course, given our understanding of brain science at that time, it is impos-sible to be certain exactly what damage Phineas incurred. However, since his accident there have been as many as 12 studies that have attempted to identify the exact journey of the tamping iron through his head. Perhaps the most recent provides us with the most accurate information. This was conducted in 1994 by Hanna Damasio and her team using Gage's skull and three-dimensional com-puter modelling techniques. They produced possible trajectories and concluded that there was one trajectory that appeared to be the most likely path given the entry and exit points identified on the skull. They even tried to account for the subtle anatomical differences that occur in each individual's brain. Even when the trajectory is accounted for accurately, though, one cannot be certain which areas have been damaged due to such individual differences. Damasio and her team compared Gage's skull with 27 normal brains and identified seven brains that had virtually identical anatomical measures to Gage's. They simulated the tamping iron's trajectory through each of these brains and found that the areas of the brain damaged were identical in all seven cases. Hence, they were confi-dent that they had located both the likely trajectory and the brain damage involved in the accident. To be precise, they identified the damaged parts as 'the anterior half of the orbital frontal cortex … the polar and anterior mesial frontal cortices … and the anterior-most sector of the anterior cingulated gyrus'.[3] However, even here there are problems since we cannot be sure how much of the damage was caused by concussion at the time of the accident and how much by the subsequent brain infections; it was impossible to deduce this from the study of his skull. Furthermore, even if we do accept that we know the precise details of the damage to his brain, we cannot be certain what effect that damage had on Gage's personality or behaviour, since he was never studied in a systematic way. There were no systematic neuropsychological assessments in those days.

Postscript

Gage's contribution went beyond that of a medical freak – his injury changed our understanding of the localisation of brain function, particularly in the frontal cortex. Gage's case also made an important contribution to brain surgery in that it opened up the possibility that major brain surgery could be performed without fatal results. The importance of the Phineas Gage case is emphasised by the fact that it is still mentioned today in approximately 60 per cent of introductory textbooks on psychology.

Although there have been cases that have come close to rivalling that of Phineas and his injury, he remains the best-known example of a person who suffered gross brain injury and survived. For this reason it's no exaggeration to say that, from that fateful September day in 1848, he was indeed the luckiest man alive. For the remaining 11 years of his life he frequently referred to himself 'as the man who lived with a hole in the head', and that's how he is likely to be remembered forevermore in the scientific literature.

1. The most comprehensive book about Phineas Gage is without doubt the exceptionally thorough work by M. Macmillan (2002) *An Odd Kind of Fame: Stories of Phineas Gage.* Cambridge, MA: MIT Press.
2. A less thorough, but equally fascinating, account of this case is by John Fleischman (2002) *Phineas Gage.* Boston: Houghton Mifflin Co.
3. Damasio, H., Grabowski, T., Frank, R., Galaburda, A. and Damasio, A. (1994) The return of Phineas Gage: clues about the brain from the skull of a famous patient. *Science* 264, pp. 1102–5.

The man who was turned on by prams and handbags

This case study involves a married man who had developed a particularly strange sexual perversion that caused him to become sexually excited by prams and handbags. This perversion had become so marked that he had been arrested on numerous occasions and charged with causing malicious damage to prams and/or handbags. A pre-frontal leucotomy was suggested as a suitable form of treatment. However, a severe form of aversion therapy was employed prior to such a drastic, irreversible procedure; this type of therapy is often characterised as a form of brainwashing and has echoes in the 'treatments' portrayed in the Anthony Burgess novel (and subsequent film) A Clockwork Orange.[1]

The problem

This is arguably a less well-known case study[2] than the others in this book, but people often find it one of the most fascinating of all, probably due to the bizarre sexual fetish involved. The patient was a 33-year-old married man who was registered as an out-patient at a psychiatric hospital. He was being assessed for a pre-frontal leucotomy, which is a brain operation that involves the surgical cutting of the nerve tracts to and from the frontal lobes. The operation is intended to relieve severe, intractable mental or behavioural problems, but has often resulted in noticeable cognitive and/or personality changes. In the history of psychosurgery (which was first employed in 1935) it was used with patients who were so psychotic that almost any change was thought to be for the good. Operations for such reasons are unheard of today.

The patient's problem involved a bizarre sexual attraction to prams and handbags. This strange behaviour seems to have started at the age of ten when he showed impulses to attack and damage prams and handbags. Sometimes this involved little more than scratching his thumbnail down the side of a handbag or pram, but there had been occasions when the attacks had been far more serious. One involved him following a woman who was pushing a pram and smearing it with engine oil. He had occasionally cut and damaged prams and, indeed, had once cut and set fire to two empty prams he had found at a railway station.

During this time he deliberately rode his motorbike towards a pram that had a baby in it; fortunately, he swerved at the last minute and narrowly avoided injuring the child within. He also liked to try to drive through muddy puddles and splash any person pushing a pram along the pavement. He had been convicted for careless driving as a result of such incidents. The police were called to a further 12 incidents and he was again charged with driving without due care and attention. He also admitted five other attacks where he had cut or scratched prams, and he was convicted of causing malicious damage.

The patient's history revealed that he had undergone a number of years of psychiatric treatment. He admitted that he had been interested in prams since the age of ten and often made several attempts per week to attack either prams or handbags. With regard to handbags, he was usually satisfied just to scratch them with his thumbnail, and since this could be done often, and without anyone noticing, he had only once got into trouble with the police for doing it. Rather than being sent to prison, he was sent on probation to a mental hospital and transferred to a neurosis unit. There, psychiatrists decided he was unsuitable for psychotherapy, was potentially dangerous and should therefore remain in a mental hospital. However, after some time he was discharged and carried on with his career of damaging prams.

The patient had undergone many hours of psychoanalytic treatment in the hope that reasons for his strange behaviour might be uncovered. During this treatment, it was suggested that his behaviour might originate in an incident during childhood when he was playing with his toy yacht at the local boating lake. He had accidentally bumped against the side of a pram with his model yacht and 'had been impressed by the feminine consternation' shown by the mother of the child in the pram. In another incident he reported he had, for some strange reason, become sexually aroused in the presence of his sister's handbag. The patient accepted the possible significance of these events and ascribed sexual symbolism to both prams and handbags. Perhaps in Freudian terms, both of these 'containers', usually used by women, may have represented either a desire for his mother or, more generally, female genitalia.

Obviously in such a case there are a number of difficult problems to resolve. If there had been no danger to children or risk of causing damage to prams then it may have been possible just to leave the patient to continue with his rather bizarre fetish; if he was doing no harm then treatment would not necessarily have been required, unless he felt, himself, that his fetish was having a serious detrimental effect on his life. Indeed, the patient in this case was married with two children, and his wife said that he was actually a very good husband and father. However, he had occasionally attacked his own children's pram and his wife's handbag, and therefore his wife was well aware of his problems.

A possible solution?

So what can psychologists offer such a patient? Although it was prams and handbags that were the primary focus of his interest, the patient was worried that he might injure any child who happened to be in a pram that he attacked. He was once more admitted to a psychiatric hospital for 18 months, but on release continued with his bizarre behaviour. After further trouble with the police, he was again placed on probation on the understanding that he accept appropriate medical treatment. It was at this stage that psychosurgery was considered. However, before this irreversible and drastic treatment was employed, psychologists suggested he might be a suitable case for aversion therapy, which is a form of behavioural therapy. Behavioural therapy was defined by Wolpe (1958) as 'the use of experimentally established laws of learning for the purposes of changing unadaptive behaviour'.[3] Aversion therapy reduces undesirable behaviour by pairing it with an undesirable, or aversive, stimulus. Most commonly this is drug-induced nausea or pain from an electric shock. Through this conditioning the aversive stimulus becomes associated with the undesirable behaviour and thus, in turn, the undesirable behaviour is suppressed. In the not-so-distant past, it was used for a variety of behaviours considered undesirable, including homosexuality.

The aim of the treatment in this particular case was to try and alter the patient's attitude to both handbags and prams by using conditioning techniques. This involved teaching him to associate handbags and prams with unpleasant sensations instead of the evidently pleasurable, erotic ones. The patient was initially very sceptical about the treatments proposed, but said that he was willing to try anything – by this time he had noticed that even adverts in newspapers and magazines for handbags and prams were turning him on!

The principles of aversion therapy are based on classical conditioning, which was first described by a Russian physiologist called Ivan Pavlov (1849–1936). During his work on the digestive systems of dogs, Pavlov noticed that the dogs salivated at the mere sight of the person who fed them. He called the dogs' salivation in response to the actual taste and smell of meat an 'unconditioned (unlearnt) response' because it occurred naturally without any prior training (the meat was thus called an 'unconditioned stimulus'). He realised that a usually neutral act, such as the ringing of a bell, could become associated with the appearance of food, thus producing salivation as a 'conditioned response' (in response to a 'conditioned stimulus'). This process is shown in Figure 11.1.

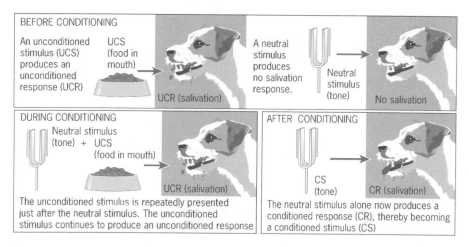

Figure 11.1: The process of classical conditioning

In later research, Pavlov found that in order for the conditioned response to be maintained, it had to be paired periodically with the unconditioned stimulus or the learned association would be forgotten (this forgetting is known as 'extinction'). Classical conditioning can be applied to human behaviour and is able to account for such complex phenomena as a person's emotional reaction to a particular song or perfume, based on a past experience with which it is associated. Classical (also called Pavlovian or associative learning) conditioning is also the basis for many different types of fears or phobias, which can occur through a process called 'stimulus generalisation' (for example, a child who has a bad experience with a particular dog may learn to fear all dogs – see Chapter 13). Classical conditioning principles have been developed into a variety of therapeutic techniques. One such is aversion therapy, the goal of which is to make the currently pleasant stimulus unpleasant.

The conditioning treatment proposed in this case involved the injection of a drug called apomorphine, which produces sickness or nausea. The prams or handbags were produced soon after the drug was given, when the nausea occurred. The prams and handbags thus represented the conditioned (learnt) stimuli and the nausea represented the unpleasant response with which the conditioned stimulus was to be associated. The treatment regime was tough. The treatment was given every two hours, day and night, and no food was allowed. At night-time amphetamines were used to keep the patient awake. At the end of the first week, treatment was suspended and he was allowed home. After eight days he was brought back into hospital to continue the treatment and he reported jubilantly that he had been able to have sexual intercourse with his wife without any of his old fantasies involving handbags or prams. His wife also said that she had noticed a marked change for the better in his behaviour. Despite this improvement, treatment was re-commenced but a different emetic (nausea-inducing drug) was used when the effect of the apomorphine became less pronounced. After another five days the patient reported that the mere sight of prams and handbags made him feel sick. He was confined to bed and given prams and handbags to play with while the treatment then continued at irregular intervals. On the evening of the ninth day he rang his bell and pleaded with the nurses to take away the prams and handbags. They refused to do so. However, a few hours later, during which time the patient had cried continuously, a doctor removed the prams and handbags and gave him a glass of milk and a sedative. The following day the patient opened up his overnight bag and gave up a number of photographs of prams to the doctor, saying that he had carried them for a year, but felt that he would no longer need them.

The patient left hospital, but continued to attend as an outpatient. After six months the doctors decided to re-admit him for a booster treatment course. He reluctantly agreed to this. The psychologists produced a film of women carrying handbags and pushing prams in the 'arousing and provocative' way he had previously described. Before the film was started he was given the emetic that had made him feel sick. He was also given handbags to play with. After this course, no further treatment was given. Eysenck reported[4] that the patient was subsequently followed up over a period of years and progressed well. He no longer fantasised about prams and handbags. His wife said that she was no longer worrying about him falling foul of the police, and that their sexual relations had improved greatly. His probation officer also reported that he was making good progress. He never got into further trouble with the police, and gained promotion at work. Eysenck reports that the treatment had been remarkably successful, both for the patient, his wife, his family and society at large.

Treatment issues

This case, and the use of aversion therapy in general, raises a number of serious problems that need to be addressed. The first involves the treatment methods used. Many people would argue that aversion therapy is not a very understanding or humane form of treatment. The approaches used often seem very mechanical and many people (including many psychologists) find it distasteful for human beings to be treated in this way. After all, there is no doubt that the treatment involved a great deal of pain and discomfort. Many believe this is a kind of brainwashing – a degrading process in which human beings are viewed as a simple 'box' of conditioned reflexes. It is argued that the use of aversion therapy devalues the individual with its premise that all humans learn in the same way and therefore can be treated and conditioned in the same way. However, Eysenck argued that, in any such argument, the alternatives to aversion therapy have to be considered.

The first option was to use some other form of psychotherapy – perhaps psychoanalysis. However, there is some evidence (particularly that reported by Eysenck himself) that this form of 'talking cure' does not have any real positive benefits. Indeed, Eysenck has even reported that Freudian psychoanalysis can have a detrimental effect. Of course, a patient might be left simply to get better over time – this effect is called 'spontaneous remission' – however, it has generally been shown that disorders of this particular type are unlikely to demonstrate a high rate of spontaneous remission. In addition, the patient in this case had already received a variety of psychiatric treatment prior to the aversion therapy, with no success whatsoever. Eysenck suggested that it was unlikely, then, that any other form of talking cure would have succeeded.

The other option would have been to sentence the patient to a lengthy prison sentence. This would have amounted to a punishment for his actions, but again there is little evidence that this form of punishment has any long-lasting beneficial effect on future actions, particularly in the case of sexual perverts. Indeed, some people have argued that prison merely has the effect of making such people far more careful to cover their tracks in the future.

Of course, one other option would have been to let him go free or put him on probation. After all, many of his behaviours were comparatively harmless and often involved little more than scratching the side of a pram with his thumbnail. However, surely members of the public do have a right to be protected from such individuals? Although the patient professed that he had no desire to harm children, this was obviously an unfortunate potential side-effect of his strange desires towards prams. In addition, some of his attacks on women's handbags had also had a very upsetting effect on the women involved. Looking at all the options available, Eysenck argued that there is a choice to be made between asking the patient to submit to a method of treatment (which is uncomfortable and unpleasant, but not for very long – although to the patient it may seem interminable), sending him to prison, allowing him to go free, or asking him to submit to a lengthy, expensive and possibly ineffective psychotherapeutic treatment in hospital.

Eysenck suggested that, given the different options available, aversion therapy was the most appropriate and, indeed, the most effective form of treatment for all concerned. Indeed, from the patient's point of view, one could debate whether it is right to prevent them from having a therapy that they themselves actively desire and/or have sought simply because some people feel it degrades the individual to some extent. This argument was developed by Eysenck. He argued that the patients themselves were the ones that underwent the therapy and they were not complaining (although, as we will see, this comment is contentious). He claimed that many people went to great lengths to seek out behavioural therapy and they should not be denied their right to treatment. He considered aversion therapy to be a safe and effective treatment for many conditions that are difficult to correct, and wrote that it was only fair to allow the ultimate decision to be made by sufferers themselves.

Of course, many people are still uneasy about using aversion therapy for conditions that do not pose any danger to society. An example of a behaviour that aversion therapy has been used to alter in the past is homosexuality. The homosexual who wishes to change his sexuality is likely to feel this way as a result of social disapproval. Such disapproval, along with peer pressure can, even today, be powerful forces that encourage a homosexual to seek aversion therapy. It may be more appropriate, though, to argue that such treatments should not be available to homosexuals and that they, rather, should be counselled as a way of helping them to accept their homosexuality and to understand that the problem in this case lies with society rather than the individual himself.

The principles involved in the 'treatment' of homosexuality[5,6] in the past typically involved showing pictures or films of naked males. These constituted the conditioned stimuli. In these experiments emetics and/or electric shocks were used as the unpleasant, or unconditioned, response. Electric shocks have a number of advantages over the use of emetics. First, the strength of the shock can be regulated accurately and the timing can be very precise too; nausea and vomiting after the injection of a drug cannot be timed as accurately as a shock. A shock can be predicted to within a second, whereas nausea sometimes takes effect over a number of minutes. According to conditioning principles the timing of the unconditioned response is particularly important for the learning process – that is, the shorter the time delay to the response, the more readily it is associated with the conditioned stimuli; this is called the law of contiguity.

One of the questions that have arisen with regard to homosexuality relates to the possibility of changing a person's sexual behaviour through the use of such therapy. One would have thought that, having been 'cured' of his sexual desire for members of the same sex, the patient would be left with no sexual desire at all. Many critics of aversion therapy argue that this is exactly what happens. However, Eysenck claimed that in the majority of cases there was an increase in interest in members of the opposite sex concomitant with the decline in interest in members of the same sex. That is, a homosexual treated along these lines was not likely to remain asexual but would, more often than not, adjust to a heterosexual lifestyle. It was reported later[7] that Eysenck did accept that, in a minority of cases, some homosexuals did become sexually dysfunctional as a result of aversion therapy.

Although Eysenck and other advocates of aversion therapy claimed a 'success' rate as high as 50 per cent, these claims were never satisfactorily supported. There are even claims that patients who were rendered asexual in response to the therapy were counted among the successful treatments. Many psychiatrists abandoned the use of aversion therapy, not out of any ethical concern for their patients or because they thought such treatment was inhumane, but because they thought it simply didn't work. It has been documented that some homosexual men who underwent aversion therapy have suffered serious long-term psychological effects, including depression, despair and attempted suicide.

Eysenck and Tatchell

As with so many contentious debates in psychology, one of the main players was a controversial figure. Hans Eysenck's lifelong combative style caused a biographer to call him the 'controversialist in the intellectual world'.[8] Eysenck was well aware of this and seemed to revel in it. He wrote,

> From the days of opposition to Nazism in my early youth, through my stand against Freudianism and projective techniques, to my advocacy of behaviour therapy and genetic studies, to more recent issues, I have usually been against the establishment and in favour of the rebels ... I prefer to think that on these issues the majority were wrong, and I was right.[9]

He certainly polarised views in both academic and non-academic audiences alike, and entitled his autobiography *Rebel With a Cause*. One prominent critic has been gay rights activist Peter Tatchell, who had a series of well-publicised confrontations with Eysenck in the 1970s and 1980s.

Tatchell and others vehemently questioned the use and 'success' of aversion therapy, particularly in the treatment of homosexuality. Tatchell reported cases where patients had become chronic depressives as a direct result of undergoing the therapy. Indeed the case of Captain Billy Clegg of the Royal Tank Regiment is often cited as an example of the negative aspects of the therapy. Clegg was arrested in Southampton in the days when homosexuality was illegal. He was sentenced to six months' compulsory aversion therapy at a local military psychiatric hospital. He died undergoing treatment and, despite his death certificate stating that he died of natural causes, there were many at the time (including medical experts) who argued that he had died from coma and convulsions as a direct result of the apomorphine injections he was given during treatment. Unfortunately, there are many other testimonies from young men who underwent similar appallingly painful and unsuccessful treatments in the 1960s under the guise of aversion therapy.

A Clockwork Orange

Parallels have frequently been drawn between the use of aversion therapy and the portrayal of similar treatments in the book and subsequent film *A Clockwork Orange*. Although many behaviourists deny the link, the treatment of the main protagonist in the book, Alex, has certain similarities with the current case. The book's author, Anthony Burgess, did indeed intend the novel to explore issues of free will and behaviourism. In the book, Alex, a teenage hooligan, is jailed for his crimes and agrees to 'aversion therapy' in order to get a reduced sentence. Once cured, he is placed back in society and subsequently rejected by his friends and relatives. At one point he breaks into the house of an author who is writing a book called *A Clockwork Orange*, in which he argues that aversion therapy should not be used since it turns people into 'clockwork oranges' (Anthony Burgess served in the Armed Forces in Malaya and 'ourang' is Malay for 'man'). The author's view was that the therapy denies people the chance to choose to be good, they thus lose their free will. Burgess wrote that it was,

> ... in Britain, about 1960, that respectable people began to murmur about the growth of juvenile delinquency and suggest [that the young criminals] were a somehow inhuman breed and required inhuman treatment ... There were irresponsible people who spoke of aversion therapy ... Society, as ever, was put first. The delinquents were, of course, not quite human beings: they were minors, and they had no vote; they were very much them as opposed to us, who represented society.[10]

Of course, the case of the 'prams and handbags' patient should not really be compared with the treatment of homosexuals. However, prior to the early 1970s, homosexuality was actually classifiable as a psychiatric disorder. At the time, many people questioned whether aversion therapy should have been given to people who were indulging in practices where no public harm was done. Further, there was the question of whether this kind of treatment should be given to individuals even if they themselves requested it. A similar dilemma exists in the treatment of body dysmorphia, a mental disorder defined as a preoccupation with a perceived defect in one's appearance. The media, as is their wont, often incorrectly refer to it as 'imagined ugliness syndrome', since the ugliness is very real to the person concerned. A form of body dysmorphia is apotemnophilia, which is the desire to have a disabled identity – thus sufferers with healthy limbs request one or two limb amputations. In cases where this has been refused some people have been driven to 'do-it-yourself amputation' where they have, say, placed an 'unwanted' limb on a railway line and awaited the consequences. Was it ethically acceptable to have refused such people surgical amputations?

In terms of homosexuality, it is frequently argued that the problem lies with society rather than the homosexual. Advocates of aversion therapy argue that patients only receive it once they have had the nature of the treatment explained to them thoroughly. They would have to give their informed consent for the treatment and will have signed a legal document to this effect. However, the therapy's opponents argue that many individuals have been virtually blackmailed into agreeing to such therapy and given little option but to sign the appropriate forms; given a choice between prison or treatment many would have 'volunteered' for the latter. It was also argued that many homosexuals may have become so ostracised as a result of society's rejection and oppression of homosexuals that they would also have volunteered, albeit unwillingly.

Aversion therapy in the laboratory has a number of disadvantages. As already mentioned, the first is that conditioned responses are subject to extinction when they are not continuously reinforced. This is why the 'prams and handbags' patient had to return for booster courses. A person's conditioned response, like all conditioned responses, changes in its degree of strength from day to day and hour to hour. This is a well-known laboratory phenomenon and has been demonstrated in dogs trained to salivate to the sound of a bell (when food has previously been paired with the sound of a bell). The change in strength is dependent on a great number of factors: the hungrier the dog, for instance, the greater the number of drops of saliva. The same can also apply to homosexuality or the case of the man who had a fetish for prams and handbags. If desire is strong at a particular moment and opportunity beckons, then people may not be so easily able to resist temptation. If this occurs, then some weakening of the conditioning process will occur and the next time they find themselves in a similar situation the temptation may be resisted less strongly: the principle of extinction will work against the therapy and in favour of the spontaneous remission of the conditioned response they have tried to replace. In other words, the conditioned response that they learned in the first place, and which constituted their disorder, may actually re-occur. In cases such as this, it is suggested that the aversive conditioning should go on well beyond the point where it has begun to take effect. This is sometimes called over-conditioning and certainly occurred in the case of the man with the fetish for prams and handbags. The patient himself said that he was cured days before he was actually allowed to leave hospital.

In practice, over-conditioning does not go on for very long, and does not continue over years. There are a number of reasons for this. The first is that it would obviously be too time consuming for both its purpose and the patient. In the second place, experiments or therapy using vomiting are messy and expensive in terms of therapeutic time. Third, the process is strenuous and unpleasant for both the experimenter and for the patient; consequently it is thought best to try to limit the therapy to as short a time period as possible. Arguably, then, for speed and strength of conditioning, it is actually more efficient to use electric shocks.

A comparison can be made between over-conditioning and the administering of booster doses – the standard medical practice for a variety of disorders. Vaccination boosters are given from time to time, against, for instance, measles. It is also standard practice in some clinics for alcoholics who have been treated with aversion therapy to be called back on an annual basis to receive short 'booster' treatments. In a way, over-conditioning could be considered to be the psychological equivalent of a booster dose.

Another interesting aspect of aversion therapy is that reinforcement works best when it's not based on total, 100 per cent, reinforcement. The most effective way to condition is to use partial reinforcement techniques. In other words, if we want to train a dog to salivate to the sound of a bell, we don't produce the meat (the unconditioned stimulus) every time the bell is sounded. A far better method is to reinforce the conditioned stimulus (the bell) on only 25 or 50 per cent of the trials. The obvious reason for this is that if the dog has been conditioned on only 25 per cent of occasions then hearing a bell and not receiving meat is not unusual – it might receive meat next time it hears a bell, thus the salivation response continues to the sound of the bell. Partial reinforcement, then, makes extinction less likely – it is much slower to take effect than it would be were 100 per cent reinforcement to be used.

The power of conditioning

This chapter has talked about the use of aversion therapy in the rather strange case of a man with a fetish for prams and handbags and also as a treatment for homosexuality. Perhaps the best example of aversion therapy though is its use as a treatment for alcoholism. It has been used in this way for a number of years; indeed, treatment of alcoholism has quite the longest history in psychology. The method used to treat alcoholism once again involves conditioning. This takes place in a quiet, darkened room, typically with a spotlight shining on a number of alcohol bottles that have been placed on a table in front of the patient. The patient is the only person present, apart from a doctor. The doctor injects a mixture of emetine, ephedrine (a stimulant to improve the conditioning process) and pilocarpine (which makes the patient sweat and salivate profusely, and thus adds to the symptoms produced by the emetine). In this way the patient is brought to the verge of nausea and vomiting, at which point any additional gastric irritation, caused by even the smallest alcoholic drink, produces nausea and vomiting immediately.

The problem with this method is that it is quite difficult to maintain a patient on the verge of vomiting, thus considerable experience is required as well as individual knowledge of the patient. Of course, between sessions the patient must be given soft drinks and water, in order to avoid the development of any aversion to, say, the handling of glasses in general or the act of drinking itself. Thousands of patients have been treated in this way, perhaps the most famous being ex-footballer George Best (although in his case it does not seem to have been entirely successful). About half the patients treated for alcoholism in this way remain alcohol-free for at least two to five years, and 25 per cent for 10 to 13 years after treatment; some require further help in the shape of subsequent treatments over a number of years. If these subsequent treatments over the years are included, the overall abstinence rate as a result of this treatment is believed to be around 51 per cent for all patients. This is an amazingly high recovery figure compared to treatment by any other method.

The case of the man turned on by prams and handbags is testimony to the power of conditioning in dealing with sexual (mal)adjustment. Reinforcement of behaviour has led to sexual norms that vary both within and between cultures. An example taken from within western cultures would include the physical shape of women. In the 1920s, for instance, the bosom was flattened as much as possible and almost denied by women. Nowadays, perhaps the reverse is true. And would Marilyn Monroe, a size 16, have become such an iconic figure today given the current trend for 'thin' women? It seems more likely that she may have been persuaded (conditioned) into dieting in order to change her shape to one that corresponded more with current tastes.

An example of the power of conditioning between cultures also involves the function of the breast. In western societies, breasts have sexual connotations. However, this is not the case in all societies. There are some societies in which breasts are seen as being merely of functional importance, for child-rearing purposes only. The South Sea Islanders, for example, could not understand the great interest shown by white sailors in the female natives' exposed breasts.

Homosexuality was removed from the list of psychiatric disorders in the 1970s, but that did not mark the end of the use of aversion therapy to treat non-conforming sexual behaviour. Although it is no longer sanctioned by the

American Psychiatric Association as an appropriate treatment for homosexuality, some therapists continue to use it, especially those involved in the reparative therapy movement, where aversion therapy has been used with paedophiles and other sex offenders. Covert sensitisation is a more humane and physically safer variation of aversion therapy that has also been used with such patients. It involves both the deviant and aversive stimuli being imagined and described to the patient, rather than actually being experienced. A similar procedure, called shame aversion therapy, involves subjecting the patient to public shame or humiliation allied to their deviant behaviour.

Studies have investigated the effectiveness of aversion therapy in the treatment of behaviours such as paedophilia, exhibitionism and transvestism. Most of these have used nausea or drug-induced sleep deprivation. In general, very few controlled studies with multiple patients have been conducted and thus no firm conclusions can be drawn as to the effectiveness of these treatments.[11]

1. Burgess, A. (1962) *A Clockwork Orange*. Harmondsworth: Penguin.
2. 'The case of the prams and handbags', reported by Eysenck, H.J. (1965) *Fact and Fiction in Psychology*. Harmondsworth: Penguin.
3. Wolpe, J. (1958) *Psychotherapy by Reciprocal Inhibition*. Stanford, Conn.: Stanford University Press.
4. Eysenck, *Fact and Fiction*.
5. King, M., Smith, G. and Bartlett, A. (2004) Treatments of homosexuality in Britain since the 1950s – an oral history: the experience of patients. *British Medical Journal* 23, p. 427.
6. King *et al.*, Treatments of homosexuality, p. 429.
7. *Guardian*, 13 September 1997.
8. Gibson, H.B. (1981) *Hans Eysenck: The Man and His Work*. London: Peter Owen.
9. Eysenck, H. (1997) *Rebel With a Cause*. New Brunswick, NJ: Transaction Publishers.
10. http://batr.org/flicks.html (accessed 22 September 2004).
11. Council on Scientific Affairs of the American Medical Association (1987) Aversion therapy. *Journal of the American Medical Association* 258(18), 13 November, pp. 2562–5.

12 | The Wild Boy of Aveyron: the story of Victor

On 9 January 1800 a young boy aged about 11 or 12 appeared from the woods sur-rounding the village of Saint-Sernin in southern France. He walked erect but could not speak and made only unintelligible cries. He wore only a tattered shirt and was completely unperturbed by his nakedness. He was caught when he entered the garden of the local tanner, intent on digging up some vegetables to eat. As is the norm in such small rural villages, word quickly spread about the capture of the 'wild savage'. So began the story of the Wild Boy of Aveyron,[1] as he was to be known – a wild child who would soon become the talk of Europe.

Discovery

The boy was described as being four and a half feet tall, with white (but tanned) skin, a roundish face, a pointed nose, dark brown matted hair and hundreds of little scars covering his entire body. In addition, he had a 41 mm scar across his throat. These scars led to speculation that he had been mistreated at some time and/or had had his throat cut before being abandoned. His right leg was bent slightly inwards, so he walked with a slight limp. It was quickly discovered that he was not housetrained – he squatted to urinate and defecated standing up, wherever he happened to be. He chose to eat only potatoes, which he threw on to an open fire and then ate scorching hot, usually burning himself in the process. It became clear to all that visited him in the early days (and there were many curious onlookers) that he had lived wild in the woods for quite some time and was completely devoid of any of the usual social niceties. After two days, the boy was taken to the local orphanage in Saint-Affrique where he was named Joseph.

Immediately, Joseph seemed to turn inwards and suffered from some kind of depression, since it was reported that he didn't make a sound for the next two weeks. He refused virtually all food, with the exception of potatoes, and would drink only water. He tore up any clothes he was given to wear and would not sleep in a bed. All his senses appeared intact but he paid little attention to any-thing with the exception of his food and sleep. The director of the orphanage realised that he had a unique case on his hands that would fascinate both scholars and lay people alike. He called the boy a 'phenomenon' and wrote to Parisian newspapers suggesting that the boy be studied and taken care of by the government. The story of the 'enfant sauvage de L'Aveyron' became the talk of Paris. Here was a chance to test the philosophical theories of Jean Jacques Rousseau ...

In his early writing, Rousseau argued that man is essentially good, a 'noble savage' when in the 'state of nature' (the state of all the other animals, and the condition man was in before the creation of civilisation and society), and that 'good' people are made unhappy and corrupted by their experiences in society. He viewed society as 'artificial' and 'corrupt', and believed that the development of society results in the continuing unhappiness of man. The discovery of a 'wild child' gave people the opportunity to test these ideas fully, to view a child who had grown up as nature intended without the 'unnatural' influences of society.

At this time in Paris there was a famous institute for deaf-mutes, which was run by Roche-Ambroise Cucurron Sicard, a respected academic and an acknowledged expert in the education of the deaf. Having read about the case, Sicard wrote two letters requesting custody of the boy for scientific study. One of these letters was to Lucien Bonaparte, Napoleon's brother, who was Minister of the Interior in the new republic. With such powerful friends, it was perhaps inevitable that the boy would eventually find himself the subject of intense scrutiny in Paris.

Nevertheless, the local commissioner suggested that the boy remain in the local vicinity for a short period so that his story could be checked for authenticity (there were fears it was a hoax) and so that local parents whose children had gone missing could come and see if he was their own child. During this time, Joseph began gradually to expand his diet, eating peas, green beans, walnuts and rye bread. After four months he started to eat meat, but appeared indifferent to whether it was cooked or raw. He used to take any leftovers out into the garden and bury them in the ground, perhaps saving them to eat later.

The years of isolation

Further details were sought about the case. There were many intriguing questions to answer. Was the boy a child of nature? Was he a real wild child or was he an imbecile who had been abandoned a few weeks earlier in the woods? Could he care for himself in the wild? How long had the boy lived wild? Where had he lived, and how?

Reports stated that a naked boy had been seen in an area around Lacaune, approximately 70 miles to the south of Saint-Sernin, for at least the previous two to three years. He survived on roots and acorns, and ran away whenever anybody tried to approach him. He was occasionally spotted moving on all fours, but was later found only to do this when very tired. The lack of marked calluses on his knees suggested that for the most part he walked upright. Apparently, peasants living in the area were aware of his existence and regarded him merely as a curiosity to be ignored. There were reports that he had once been captured, in 1798, and put on show in the village square, but he had escaped and was not sighted again for at least a year. Then, in June 1799, three hunters accidentally came upon him and captured him. A local widow looked after him for a few weeks; she taught him how to cook potatoes and gave him a shirt to wear – the same tattered shirt he had been found in months later. After the kindness shown by the widow, the boy appeared to seek out more human contact and was frequently spotted by local farmers. He would often approach isolated farms and wait nearby for food to be given to him. One farmer regularly gave him potatoes, which he would cook in a fire, then pick them out and eat them burning hot. After being fed, he would disappear once again into the hills to hide out in the most isolated of spots.

In effect, the farmers treated him as one might a wild animal or bird that visits occasionally. Although they recognised him as human they did not feel they should try to capture or clothe him. He was causing them no harm so they saw no reason to try to tame him. In those days, people were more familiar with the idea of 'village idiots' roaming among them, and the wild boy must to them have fallen into some such category of humanity. The boy could probably have continued to live such an existence, but for some reason chose to move north, up to Saint-Sernin. The people there were less familiar with his presence and thus his capture was far more likely. The local commissioner spent some weeks trying to find out what had happened to the boy in the first place but there was no reliable evidence to explain how he had ended up living abandoned in the forest. Subsequently there have been many far-fetched tales associated with him having being brought up by wolves and such like, but these remain pure conjecture.

In order to investigate further whether he was a hoax or not, Joseph was tested on a number of rather crude experiments. For example, he was given a mirror to see what his reaction would be. He saw the image of a boy but apparently did not recognise it as himself. Indeed, he tried to reach out and grasp the potato he saw in the mirror.

There were also doubts as to whether he could have survived the harsh winters found in that area of France. Although the summers there were hot, winters were cold with many nights below freezing and accompanied by frequent snowfalls. Furthermore, the boy seemed to dislike the cold since he chose to spend many hours curled up by the fire. To test his tolerance to cold, the boy was stripped and led by the hand outdoors on a freezing evening. He showed no hesitation and even seemed to enjoy his naked foray in the cold. It was concluded that, much like a cat or a dog, he was largely indifferent to the cold but, given the choice, would prefer to spend time warming himself by the fire.

Sent for further study in Paris

After five months in the local district, the boy had made little real progress. The people responsible for his care were discouraged and suggested that he was still more of an animal than a human. It was decided that the best solution would be to send him to Paris for further training. Unfortunately he caught smallpox on the journey to the capital, which delayed his arrival, but eventually, on 6 August 1800, his stagecoach arrived outside the institute for deaf-mutes sited in the Luxembourg Gardens. He was immediately handed over into the charge of Sicard. For the first two weeks, Sicard was so busy with other work that Joseph was virtually abandoned once more. He had grown quite fat by this time, loved to be tickled and was often found laughing although no one could be sure what he was laughing at. However, these apparent signs of progress were tempered by less promising behaviour. Joseph would still not use a toilet but would go outside and perform his bodily functions without any modesty. He was interested almost exclusively in eating and sleeping. Indeed, it was reported that 'his entire being was focused in his stomach'. He paid virtually no attention to anything around him and took no interest in anything either. He had become almost completely apathetic. He actively avoided other children at the institute but was never mean or nasty towards others.

There are conflicting reports at this time as to whether Joseph was given free rein in the institute. Some reports suggest that he was left almost entirely to his own devices and that he never tried to escape (which must have been possible for him); others say that he was frequently chained around the waist in order to prevent his escape attempts. Whichever was the case, nothing seems to have been done for Joseph for three months, during which time his condition deteriorated. He began soiling his bed and started to self-harm, and to bite and scratch his helpers. He was often visited by curious members of the public who managed to bribe the attendants in order to view 'the wild child'. Joseph was continuously pestered by these onlookers, and wandered the corridors and garden of the institute in a pitiful state. Sicard, the 'great educator', appears to have ignored his charge. From being the talk of the nation, Joseph became a forgotten and abandoned child once more. It is surmised that Sicard had decided he was a hopeless case beyond help and that, by attempting to treat him, he risked ruining his own great reputation. A further commission was set up systematically to measure and ascertain Joseph's abilities. Their conclusion was the same as Sicard's: Joseph was an 'idiot', reduced to animal instincts from his time in the woods, and nothing could be done for him.

If such a child was discovered today (as in the case of Genie, in Chapter 1) they would be the subject of a whole battery of psychological tests to try to work out what deficits they had and what the possible causes were. There might be an 'organic' cause, where the deficits occur due to a physical cause such as brain injury, or a 'functional' cause, where there is no obvious physical cause. A functional explanation would suggest that environmental circumstances resulted in the deficits, whereas an organic cause would suggest a deficit at birth. In many respects, these differences mirror the nature–nurture argument discussed in relation to the case of Genie. Was Joseph born with an 'organic' problem or were his problems the result of his restricted upbringing? Given the scarcity of reliable information on the case, there can be no definitive answer to this. However, apart from the scar on his neck, which suggested that he had either scratched himself very severely in the wild or that someone had tried to cut his throat before abandoning him, there were no signs of physical injury. In 1967 Bruno Bettelheim[2] examined this case and concluded that Joseph probably suffered from a form of autism, although it was impossible to establish whether he was born with the condition (and that this contributed to his abandonment) or had developed it during his years of isolation. However, other distinguished experts in the field consider it unlikely that either an autistic boy or an 'idiot' would have managed to survive alone in the woods for five or six years. Indeed, it could be argued that a pre-adolescent boy who managed to survive alone in the woods for that many years must possess a remarkably *high* level of intelligence (it is, of course, recognised that autistic individuals can be very intelligent).

Hope

With his life going nowhere, hope arrived for Joseph in the autumn of 1800, in the shape of a new doctor who had been recruited to the institute – his name was Jean-Marc Gaspard Itard. Itard immediately took an interest in Joseph and began to watch his behaviour closely. He obviously spotted some promise in the boy that the other academics had failed to see, and started a programme of assessment and training with him. Itard secured an apartment within the institute, which enabled him to work ever more closely with Joseph. He was an enthusiastic and young doctor who was open to new ideas and innovative methods of treatment. With no family of his own, he devoted his entire life to his work and eventually, on his death, left his entire estate to benefit future generations of deaf-mutes at the institute. Itard unofficially became Joseph's foster father and devoted more and more time to the boy. In some respects, he was challenging the diagnoses of his mentors. In contrast to Sicard, Itard believed there *was* some hope for Joseph and to Sicard's credit he was willing to allow Itard the chance of proving him wrong. Itard believed that people were the product of their environment, so assumed that it was possible to re-educate Joseph given the appropriate circumstances. If this could be done, then the 'tabula rasa', or 'blank slate', theory of human development would gain support. This theory suggests that infants are born with very few innate capabilities and that development occurs almost exclusively as a result of environmental influences. It is very much the 'nurture' side of the traditional nature–nurture philosophical argument.

Itard recognised that he couldn't devote all his time to Joseph. He felt it was essential to secure help from another adult who could also become a surrogate parent. Madame Guerin lived with her husband at the institute. He worked in the gardens and they both lived in a small apartment near the kitchens, which happened to be directly below the room allocated to Joseph. The Guerins were both in their forties with grown-up children who no longer lived with them. Madame Guerin was a kindly and sympathetic person with great compassion, who was entirely undaunted by Joseph's strange behaviours. She was recruited by Itard as another surrogate parent and, remarkably, devoted the next 27 years of her life to Joseph. Joseph began to spend most of his time with Madame Guerin; she fed him, clothed him, nursed him, took him on trips out of the institute and looked after every one of his often unique needs. Given such a close relationship, any credit for the improvement in Joseph's behaviour must be shared by both Itard and Madame Guerin.

Rehabilitation

Itard designed a therapeutic programme for Joseph with the express purpose of improving his ability to speak, think and interact with others. Together, Itard and Madame Guerin started to improve the care that Joseph had experienced since his arrival at the institute. They gave him a freer rein in his activities. He loved to go for walks in the surrounding fields, particularly in bad weather, and he always chose to go to bed when it got dark. Often during the night of a full moon he would stand and stare at the countryside for hours on end out of his bedroom window. Like many so-called 'wild children' he also enjoyed snow. One morning he showed his pleasure at finding snow on the ground by going and rolling in it while laughing joyously.

During his first miserable months at the institute, Joseph had shown little interest in anything except food, he had never responded to any sound except those connected with food and, despite his wretched life, he had never been known to cry. Itard decided that just as young children benefit from water play in a daily bath, Joseph should have a hot bath every day. The regime seemed to have an immediate effect. He appeared to look forward to the baths and enjoyed pouring water over himself. Gradually he began to refuse to get into the bath if the water wasn't hot enough and thus appeared to have learnt to dislike the cold. This had two effects: first, he stopped wetting his bed at night and, second, he began to put on warm clothes to suit the temperatures found in mid-winter Paris. Other improvements were immediate too. Joseph began dressing himself and started using a spoon to get his favourite food, boiled potatoes, out of the hot pan. Itard suggests that his sense of smell started to develop and, remarkably, he saw Joseph sneeze for what he believed was the first time ever. Although Itard could not have been certain of this, Joseph's frightened response to his sneeze supports the idea that he had never done this before. Joseph also grew quite fastidious about his food and after years of living wild in the most filthy manner imaginable, he became somewhat obsessive about dirt. He refused plates of food if he thought there was anything even slightly amiss with them. When Joseph started catching colds and other minor ailments, Itard declared ironically that the civilising process was working!

Itard also set about developing Joseph's mental faculties. As was the case with Virginia Axline and her treatment of Dibs almost 200 years later (Chapter 5), Itard placed a great deal of importance on the role of play in developing Joseph's intelligence. However, he was disappointed at Joseph's lack of interest in many of the toys he was given and, indeed, Joseph often hid or destroyed them when given the chance. One game he did enjoy involved hiding objects under upturned cups and then mixing up the cups to see which one contained the object. Initially, to gain his interest, Itard used a chestnut, which Joseph would then eat. Joseph soon became extremely skilled at following the moves, again suggesting that an untapped level of intelligence lay beneath the surface.

One day, Itard took Joseph out into the countryside on a two-day trip in a horse-drawn carriage. In marked contrast to his lack of interest in the views on his journey to Paris some months previously, Joseph seemed ecstatic to be out in the woods and fields once again. He jumped from side to side, soaking up the images of the countryside as it sped past. Itard was so worried by this rediscovered interest that precautions were taken to prevent Joseph's escape back into the wild. On his return to the institute, Itard reported Joseph as being more troubled than ever and vowed never to take him back into the country-side again. Madame Guerin continued to take him on daily walks in the next-door garden of an observatory and Joseph settled down again to a routine approximating to family life. Madame Guerin reports that he was generally happy.

Learning to communicate

Of course, Joseph still did not communicate with anyone. Despite being able to hear, he paid no real attention to any sounds bar the occasional response to an unexpected noise or strange tone of voice. He made no real sounds beyond some suppressed cries, but he did laugh. Itard knew that Joseph could hear because if he heard voices he could quickly work out where they were coming from and run away in the opposite direction to hide. He also seemed particularly respon-sive to the sound 'O'. For this reason, Itard proposed renaming Joseph with a name that ended in this sound. From then on he was called Victor (pronounced 'Victo' in French, with the emphasis on the second syllable) and whenever he was later called by name he did acknowledge it.

Despite some improvements in his hearing there was no noticeable improve-ment in Victor's speech. After various experiments, it was concluded that he was capable of producing speech and that his slit throat had not affected his vocal chords. Itard spent many frustrating months trying to encourage Victor to speak. Victor would only drink water and milk ('lait') and every time he was given water or milk Itard pronounced the appropriate word over and over again, hoping that Victor would associate one of his favourite sounds with the drink. After hundreds of such trials, Victor did indeed articulate the word 'lait' when milk was poured, but despite Itard's efforts he never said the word *before* he received milk, only on *presentation* of the milk. Itard concluded that Victor never really grasped the word's true meaning – he had simply associated the sound with the drink. Despite Itard's disappointment, Victor did make some progress with spoken language. He began to copy Madame Guerin's common saying 'Oh God' ('Oh Dieu'), at least to the extent that it was recognisable as such. Itard also proposed that Victor's actions were so highly expressive by this time that he had little need for speech. Victor had little difficulty in expressing his wishes: pointing to the outside meant he wanted to go for a walk and getting out his cup meant that he wanted milk. If visitors bored him, Victor would go and get their gloves and hat to hasten their departure. What words could be clearer than that!

Despite housing about a hundred deaf-mutes, who communicated with each other on a daily basis using sign language, there is no evidence that Victor was given any training in this 'action' language. Modern speech therapists have argued that Victor might have readily responded to such teaching. Itard gave no indication why this path was not chosen but instead developed another method of teaching that involved hanging objects beneath simple line drawings representing them. Itard would then take away the drawings and get Victor to replace them beside the appropriate object. Victor soon managed to learn what was required of him, even if the objects were moved around the room. He was definitely developing the capacity to 'compare and contrast' objects and drawings.

The next stage was to get him to distinguish colours and shapes using a similar procedure whereby coloured pieces of paper of various shapes were fastened round his bedroom. Again, Victor quickly managed to group the paper cut-outs by both shape and colour. Itard pressed on, making the tasks more difficult day by day. Rather than finding this a challenge to be overcome, Victor appeared to get increasingly frustrated. It became almost a battle of wills between the two of them, with Itard forcing the pace and Victor becoming ever more perplexed at being asked to perform tasks that he clearly thought were beyond him. Victor's usual response was to fly into a rage and throw objects around the room. One day Victor became so enraged at the task he was asked to do that he started to bite the fireplace, throw burning coals around the room and have an epileptic fit that resulted in him losing consciousness. At this point, Itard backed off from these tasks, but this resulted in Victor having more frequent attacks at the slightest frustration. Itard became very worried for Victor. He wondered whether he was beginning to have the fits as a remedy to any frustration, whether the fits were becoming a learnt habit as a form of self-protection. Itard decided to take drastic action. One day when Victor was just beginning to show the initial signs of having a 'fit', Itard grabbed him by the hips and dangled him out of the fifth-floor window head first. After a few seconds he pulled him back inside and Victor stood there trembling, pale and in a cold sweat. Itard made him pick up the work that he had thrown around the room and then Victor lay down quietly on his bed and cried. It was the first time Itard had seen him cry. This threat from Itard had a remarkable effect and the now 'tamed' Victor continued with his work with far less resistance; his full-scale tantrums never returned.

Over the next few months, Itard reported that Victor learnt to spell simple words and to understand that words stood for 'objects'. Sometimes he even carried around letters with him to spell out his needs. For example, he once took the letters L A I T and placed them on a table to get a glass of milk. Itard was excited at this progress. He developed a mantra, 'education is all', arguing that with love, patience and understanding, and the systematic use of rewards and punishments human beings are capable of quite remarkable feats. Psychologists might compare some of Itard's methods to 'operant conditioning' techniques (which, put simply, means 'learning through the consequences of one's actions'). But Itard predominantly adopted a sympathetic, humane approach, which recognised the individual needs of Victor. Perhaps a more appropriate comparison of his individually tailored learning methods would be with what we now call 'special education'.

Victor obviously valued both Madame Guerin and, perhaps to a lesser extent, Itard. Stories have been recounted about Victor crying for long periods when he knew he had upset her. Itard also reports going to Victor's bed before he was asleep and being welcomed by hugs, laughter and kisses, then being invited to sit on the bed with him. It had taken Itard nine painstaking months to get to this stage, but he had certainly made some noticeable progress with Victor against all the perceived wisdom at the time.

Development of other faculties

Itard decided to continue to try to develop some of Victor's faculties, including his hearing, speech and taste. He developed a method whereby he blindfolded Victor to see if he could discriminate between different musical sounds and words. Despite Victor's ability to make such discriminations and the fact that his hearing was intact, after months of teaching, he had managed to make only minimal progress. This involved learning a few simple monosyllabic words to identify anger or friendship. Itard became dispirited and began to reassess Victor's progress. Victor's ability to spell out the word 'lait' was hailed as his greatest cognitive achievement, but Itard noticed that he could really only regularly use the word on immediate presentation of milk. As with his speech, he still couldn't use the word 'lait' to indicate that he wanted milk. Itard concluded that without this Victor could not be said to possess real language capacity. Itard also discovered that Victor could not imitate. He set up two blackboards side by side and tried to get Victor to copy his movements, Victor found it impossible. This inability to imitate must have severely affected his learning capacity and also tells us something of his capabilities. Many non-human animals can imitate behaviour successfully and yet Victor could not.

However disheartened Itard was over this setback he did not give up on his teachings with Victor. He began sending Victor out of the room to fetch objects that he had put in other rooms. After a lot of training, Victor could go to another room and collect as many as four objects that Itard had shown him on cards. This was reported as a clear sign of developing cognitive ability, but later Itard sent Victor to a room and asked him to collect a book. Despite the room having many books in it Victor could not link the word 'book' with *any* book, only the *specific* book with which he had associated the word in the first place. He could not generalise the words on the cards presented to him with any object, only one specific object. Again Itard reports this as an incredibly dispiriting result, so dispiriting in fact that Itard called him a 'useless being'. Despite not understanding a word that he said, Victor must have sensed the tone of the message, closed his eyes and started sobbing. Itard went and hugged Victor, as any father might, and he reports that this physical moment of contact between boy and man helped their working relationship in the months to come. Eventually, Victor did learn to understand that one word could represent many similar objects and, in fact, started generalising too much, confusing the word 'brush' for 'broom', 'knife' and 'razor'. Despite setbacks, slow progress was made.

Victor began to learn more and more nouns ('room', 'person') and started to combine them with simple adjectives (such as 'big', 'small') and also verbs (such as 'touch', 'drink'). Victor even managed to write simple words that were legible, and Itard reported that, by the end of 1803, he could communicate through writing and reading in a very basic and crude way. By this time, Victor had learnt to imitate behaviour, so Itard spent months trying to get him to form the shapes of sounds with his mouth in order to facilitate his speech. Although Itard spent a long time pursuing this approach, in the end he abandoned any such attempts and concluded that Victor would never be capable of spoken language. Itard had to accept that no amount of training could overcome Victor's early deficits and this led him to question whether environmental influences (five years of training in this case) could overcome either nature or early environmental influences.

Civilised or wild?

So was Victor now a civilised, mute child or was he still basically the wild child who had been found all those years ago near Saint-Sernin? He never lost his immense enthusiasm for the beauty of nature – the sight of a full moon on a still summer's evening could leave him in raptures, and he continued to adore his daily walks with a fierce passion. Such behaviour could be interpreted in different ways: were these responses an indication of the remains of the wild child within him or did he now recognise, as a result of the civilising process, the beauty of nature?

Victor continued to live with the Guerins and seemed keen to contribute to the running of the household. He made himself useful by performing small chores such as chopping wood and laying the table. One day, Monsieur Guerin fell ill and a few days later died. The day he died, Victor set his place at the table as usual. On seeing this, Madame Guerin burst into tears. Realising that his actions had caused her tears, Victor removed the table setting and never laid it again. Such actions suggest that he was developing emotional maturity – he could understand another's feelings and empathise with them. Soon after Monsieur Guerin's death, Madame Guerin became ill and could not look after Victor. As a result, Victor escaped from the institute and was found by local police in a nearby village. It took two weeks for him to be identified and returned to the institute. On being reunited with the now recovered Madame Guerin he was ecstatically happy – he was reported as being like a son returned to his affectionate mother.

Soon after this incident, Itard decided to test Victor's sense of justice. Rather cruelly, he decided to punish Victor unfairly as a test of his understanding of right and wrong. One day after Victor had been working well at his books for quite some time, Itard suddenly rubbed out his writing, grabbed him and started to drag him over to a wardrobe where he occasionally confined him as a punishment. Victor immediately physically resisted the punishment and indeed bit Itard's hand so hard that he left toothmarks. Itard had never known Victor to resist in such a way given that on all previous occasions the punishment had been justified. Itard was delighted – he reports that the pain from the bite brought joy to his heart. The act of legitimate retaliation was proof that Victor understood and had a sense of justice and injustice – right from wrong. To Itard this was evidence of a civilising effect and a sign of Victor changing from a boy to a man. Victor was so sure of his sense of right or wrong that he would go so far as to challenge the authority of his teacher.

At this time, Victor was approximately 17 years old and Itard was anticipating a marked change in his behaviour due to puberty and an interest in all matters sexual. Victor had led a life of isolation away from the other children in the institute and had had no peers to guide his sexual conduct. Given no such guidance from Itard or Madame Guerin either, he must have been at a complete loss at what to make of his developing sexual desires. It was reported that he caressed women, hugged them and sometimes grabbed them to his neck; these behaviours must have been extremely embarrassing for the women concerned, and confusing for Victor. Indeed, he often fell into foul moods as a result of such interactions. Itard and Madame Guerin arranged special diets, cold baths and lots of exercise to ease the effects of puberty and, after some time, it seems that Victor gave up with his efforts towards the opposite sex.

The end of his training

By 1805, Itard had been training and teaching Victor for five years. It is probably fair to surmise that both Itard and Victor were fatigued by their efforts and needed a break. Madame Guerin was given official charge of Victor in 1806 and a salary of 150 francs a year to look after him. In 1810, Sicard wrote a report about Victor, detailing that his original diagnosis of 'complete idiocy' had been correct and that virtually no progress had been made in the case. This seems unfair to both Itard's and Victor's efforts and achievements; it also hastened Victor's exit from the institute. By 1811, the institute had become an all-male establishment and the administrators felt that Madame Guerin should leave her residence within the grounds and find a house nearby. They also regarded Victor as a hopeless case and a disturbing influence on the other children. Madame Guerin was given an additional 500 francs to facilitate her departure and she moved with Victor into a small house on the Impasse de Feuillantines, just around the corner from the institute. One purpose of this was to be close by so that Itard could continue to work with Victor if he so wished. However, for reasons that are not clear, this did not happen and Victor became a forgotten man once more.

There are very few reports about Victor or Madame Guerin's lives after leaving the institute. We know that Victor continued to live with Madame Guerin and there is no record of him causing any problems or scandals. It is reported that people recognised him by his limp. We don't know what he did with his life or whether he managed to earn any sort of living. Being mute, this would have been a difficult task, but Madame Guerin's annual salary would have kept them from being penniless. Victor died in 1828 at the age of 40, not an old age even in those days. There are no documents that detail cause of death or place of burial. Victor Hugo lived just four doors away for two years, but there are no clear-cut references in any of his writings to the wild boy's existence, suggesting that Victor kept himself very much to himself. The fact that he continued to live in the back streets of Paris suggests that he did not miss his former life in the deepest countryside.

Itard continued to work at the institute and developed a number of teaching techniques used successfully with deaf-mutes, which were evolved from his work with Victor. He pursued a successful career and became a respected and acknowledged expert with the deaf. At the end of his career, he worked with an up-and-coming academic called Edouard Seguin. Seguin was hugely impressed by Itard's approach and later developed special education programmes for the mentally retarded. Maria Montessori, an Italian psychiatrist, was in turn influenced by Seguin and founded Montessori schools that, even today, use cut-out shapes and letters in classes in a similar way that Itard did with Victor. Both Montessori and Seguin acknowledge their debt to Itard. There have also been criticisms of Itard's approach, though. Although he did not do it deliberately, Itard placed Victor in an isolated environment away from his peers. This excluded him from a potentially vital form of peer learning and an important means of social interaction. It seems Victor was destined to spend his entire life in some form of restricted isolation. It is also argued that Itard should have attempted to teach him sign language. It is unclear whether this would have been successful, but it has been so in other subsequent, but less profound, cases.

Postscript

What can we conclude from the case of Victor? Case studies of wild children like him should make an important contribution to the nature–nurture debate, but as has been found with subsequent case studies, there is always confusion as to whether deficits were present at birth or arose as a result of the period of isolation. In Victor's case, there are conflicting views. The idea that Victor was born an 'idiot' (to use Sicard's description), incapable of showing any real progress, can be largely discounted. Victor did make progress with Itard and surviving alone in the woods for the period of time he did without capture, would surely have required a ready and quick intelligence. Alternatively, Victor may have suffered from some psychological deficit or abuse prior to his abandonment, and his physical and mental capabilities may have been affected as a result of his years of isolation.

It remains unclear which of these two explanations carries the most weight. Itard believed in the latter and spent almost five years of his life trying to surmount the effects of Victor's isolation. It remains a contentious judgement as to whether he was successful or not, since we cannot imagine, let alone prove, what the effects of seven years of living alone in the wild would do to a young child. Additionally, with no base level of assessment of Victor's abilities it is impossible to measure the actual improvement. Evidence suggests that Victor was not born an 'idiot', but that he may have had some special needs such as a form of autism. There are many different types of autism, but it is generally a developmental disability that significantly affects both verbal and non-verbal communication and social interaction.

Victor's period of isolation certainly had a profound effect on his physical, emotional and social development. It is clear that childhood is a critical period for the learning of many skills, not least language, but that some of these deficits can be overcome as a result of intensive training later. The story of Victor is one of the most famous case studies (along with Genie – see Chapter 1) of a deprived child.[3] There are many other children recovered from the wild, girls as well as boys, that provide further evidence of the effects of deprivation and the lack of normal socialisation. These range from a child brought up by dogs, found as recently as 2004 in Siberia, to a boy who was found in 1945 living with ostriches![4]

Many of these case studies have fuelled the debate about what it is to be 'human'. Although all were born and could be categorised as *homo sapiens*, there is something more that is required before one can really be said to possess all the characteristics of what we mean by the term 'human being'. Babies are born with great potential, but need a nurturing environment in order to learn to be 'human'. Children who are deprived of this through early isolation and abuse find it extremely difficult, if not impossible, to overcome the effects at a later stage. The story of Victor illustrates this all too clearly.

A postscript to the success (or otherwise) of the Wild Boy of Aveyron case was penned by Itard himself 20 years later. Itard reported that,

> ... a large proportion of my days for six years was sacrificed to this demanding experiment. The boy ... did not gain from my attentions all the advantages I had hoped. But the numerous observations I was able to make, the instructional procedures ... [were] not entirely lost, and later I put them to more successful use in dealing with children whose muteness arose from less insurmountable causes.

1. The two most comprehensive (and recommended) books devoted to this single case study are: Roger Shattuck (1980) *The Forbidden Experiment*. London: Quartet Books, and Harlan Lane (1976) *The Wild Boy of Aveyron*. Cambridge, Mass.: Harvard University Press. The latter includes detailed verbatim accounts of the case.
2. Bettelheim, B. (1967) *The Empty Fortress*. New York: Free Press.
3. The case of two girls called Amala and Kamala, found living with wolves in India in 1920, is perhaps equally famous and is reported in Candland, D.K. (1993) *Feral Children and Clever Animals: Reflections on Human Nature*. Oxford: Oxford University Press.
4. Further amazing stories about wild children can be found on the comprehensive website www.feralchildren.com.

13 | Two little boys: the story of Little Albert and Little Peter

The history of psychology is littered with accounts of academics contesting the merits of their respective theories, with which they seek fully to explain all facets of human behaviour. One such academic, called J.B. Watson, proposed a scientific, objective psychology of behaviour called 'behaviourism'. He argued that learning should be studied without any reference to internal mental processes. He rejected the idea of introspection and instead focused on observable behaviour and how an organism (human and/or animal) learns through adaptation to their environment; in terms of the classic nature–nurture philosophical argument, the emphasis was placed very much on 'nurture'. Ivan Pavlov, working in Russia, had already shown the effect of conditioning on simple behaviours such as the salivation response in dogs, but Watson suggested that more complex human behaviours might also easily be conditioned. In order to test this hypothesis, he decided to take an 11-month-old infant and try to condition a fear response in the child, one evoked from a previously neutral stimulus. So began one of the most cited case studies in the history of psychology: the testing of Little Albert.

Background to the study

John Broadus ('J.B.') Watson originally started his work by concentrating on learning in (non-human) animals but, by 1916, had turned his attentions to human infants. Initially interested in the use of conditioned reflexes as a method of testing the senses in infants, he began to write about the conditioning of human fears. He had noticed his own children's seemingly unlearned fear of thunder and lightning, and began to consider methods by which he might condition such fears in a laboratory experiment. His first attempts to inhibit a child's reaching response to a lit candle had taken over 150 trials (mainly, he argued, because he had to stop the child from burning their hand severely) and so was not a particularly effective demonstration of the power of conditioning.

Although no one is certain exactly when the so-called 'Little Albert' study took place, it seems clear that it was some time around the Christmas of 1919.

The results of the study were co-published by Watson in 1920 with his assistant Rosalie Rayner.[1] They suggested that the complex range of human emotions shown by adults must be the result of learning through their environment. They set out to demonstrate this in an experimental demonstration with an 11-month-old infant whom they named 'Albert B.'. Albert was described as a 'normal' child, well developed for his age, with a phlegmatic character described as 'stolid and unemotional'. He had been chosen by Watson and Rayner simply because he was readily available for study (his mother was a wet-nurse at a local home for invalid children) and because, being such a strong and stable character, they felt he would come to 'relatively little harm' as a result of the study. The use of such phrases suggests they were aware at the outset that *some* harm might befall him.

At the age of nine months, Albert was put through a battery of emotional tests. He was also shown a white rat, rabbit, dog, monkey, face masks, cotton wool and a burning newspaper to gauge his reactions. His responses to these stimuli were filmed and at no time did he show any fear in any of the situations in which he was placed. During the testing it was noticed that he rarely cried, so because Watson and Rayner needed to test his fear reaction, it was necessary for them to devise a method of inducing fear in him. Possibly drawing on his own children's reactions to thunder, Watson developed a technique whereby one of the researchers, without warning, would strike a hammer on a four-foot-long steel bar suspended just behind Albert and out of his view. This procedure had the desired effect. Albert immediately showed distress at this unanticipated unpleasant sound; his breathing became stilted, his hands were flung upwards and his lips trembled. By the third stimulation, 'the child broke into a sudden crying fit'.[2]

Questions to consider

In their journal article, Watson and Rayner stated that they then spent two months deliberating over the procedure to adopt in their study. They were clearly worried about the possible effects of their experiment on Albert. Nevertheless, they decided that many of the fear reactions they were going to induce may have occurred naturally in the normal 'rough and tumble of the home'.[3] So with Albert now aged 11 months and three days they began their series of groundbreaking experiments.

The questions they set out to test were as follows. Could they condition fear of an animal by presenting it visually at the same time as striking the steel bar? Would any such conditioned emotional response transfer to other animals?

How long might such a response last? Further, what methods might be devised for removal of the response if it did not extinguish immediately?

As a test of the first question, they presented Albert with a white rat from a basket. Showing no fear, Albert reached out for the rat with his left hand and, just as he touched the rat, one of the researchers struck the steel bar with the hammer, just behind his head. He jumped violently and buried his face in the mattress. After a short period of time, he again reached out for the rat and the procedure was repeated. Albert fell forward and began to whimper. Watson and Rayner reported that, 'in order not to disturb the child too seriously, no further tests were given for one week'.[4] Exactly seven days later the rat was presented without sound. With Albert making no attempt to reach for the rat, they moved it closer. Albert instantly withdrew his hand. It was clear that his behaviour had been modified after just two presentations, and this effect had lasted a week. They gave Albert building blocks to play with to check that he had not been conditioned to fear any object given to him and he showed no fear, playing with them in the usual way. The blocks were then cleared away and five presentations of the rat and the sound were conducted, with Albert showing various levels of distress on each occasion. After these presentations, when the rat was presented to him on its own, Albert cried, turned sharply and crawled away at great speed. So fast, in fact, that they barely had time to catch him before he fell off the edge of the table on which he was sitting! As Watson and Rayner reported, it 'was as convincing a case of a completely conditioned fear response as could have been theoretically pictured'.[5] This had taken just seven joint presentations (of the rat and the sound) over a seven-day period. They had found the answer to their first question: it *is* possible to condition fear of an animal by presenting it visually along with an unpleasant, unexpected and unexplained sound.

It seems clear that Albert had acquired a conditioned (or learnt) emotional (fear) response. Before the conditioning trials, he had shown no fear of the rat, which thus represented a neutral stimulus. The striking of the steel bar was an unconditioned stimulus (US) since it naturally provoked a fear response (an unconditioned response, or UR) in Albert. With repeated presentations of the rat and the unpleasant sound, the sight of the rat alone became a conditioned stimulus (CS) and produced a learnt fear response (conditioned response, or CR) in Albert. This classical conditioning[6] procedure is summarised in Figure 13.1.

Another five days later, Little Albert found himself back in the experimental room. He played happily with his building blocks, which showed there had been no transfer of fear to other objects, such as the room, the table or the blocks. The rat was presented and he showed the conditioned fear response. To test whether there had been any transferring of the response to other animals, a

Before conditioning	During conditioning	After conditioning
Albert showed no fear of rat (neutral stimulus)	Rat (CS) is paired with unpleasant sound (US) that naturally produces fear response in Albert	Albert shows fear (CR) of rat alone (CS)

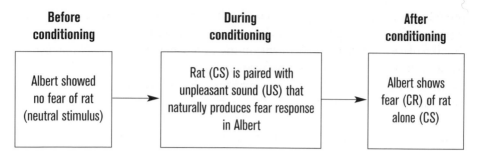

Figure 13.1: The classical conditioning of Little Albert

rabbit was presented. Albert reacted at once. He leaned as far away as possible and started to whimper and cry. When the rabbit was placed next to him, he crawled away as he had done from the rat. After a period during which he was given his building blocks to play with, a dog was presented. Albert's reaction was described as not being as pronounced as to the rabbit but still resulted in him crying. Other objects were tested. These included a fur coat made of seal skin (crying and crawling away), cotton wool (markedly less shock and fear shown) and a Santa Claus mask. One of the researchers also put his head down to see if Albert would show fear of his hair. (An aversive response was shown to the mask but less so to the presentation of the hair.) Watson and Rayner had found the answer to their second question: the conditioned fear response *did* transfer or generalise to other animals and, indeed, some similar-looking objects.

Yet again, after a period of another five days, Little Albert returned to the small, experimental room to be placed on the mattress on top of the table. Watson and Rayner decided to strengthen his fear reaction to the dog and rabbit, so paired the presentation of these animals with the striking of the steel bar. Albert was then taken to another larger room, lit with natural sunlight. They wanted to test whether his reactions would be the same in a different situation from the original experimental setting. They presented Albert on separate occasions with the rat alone, the rabbit alone and the dog alone. On each presentation, they reported a slight fear reaction but, as they describe it, it did not seem as marked as Albert's reactions in the original experimental setting. The experimenters then decided to 'freshen up the reaction to the rat' by pairing it with the sound. After a single presentation of the rat and sound in this new environment, Albert showed a fear response to presentations of both the rat and the rabbit separately. On initial presentation of the dog, he did not show such a marked fear reaction but when it was only about six inches from Albert's face, the previously mute dog barked very loudly three times. Watson and Rayner note that this produced a marked fear response in both Albert (immediate wailing) and all the experimenters present! Watson and Rayner concluded that emotional transfers do take place and are not dependent on the experimental setting. They next set about testing how long such a response might last.

Watson and Rayner stated that they knew that Albert was due to leave the hospital in one month and that this, therefore, was the longest period for which they could test how long the response would last. During this month, Albert was given no further conditioning trials, although he was given weekly developmental tests such as those concerned with handedness (testing left or right hand preferences). Three weeks after his first birthday, Albert was re-tested on his emotional responses to the previously conditioned stimuli. On presentation of the Santa Claus mask he withdrew from it and, on being 'forced to touch it', whimpered and cried. On presentation of the seal-skin coat, he withdrew his hands immediately and also began to whimper; when it was moved closer to him, he tried to kick it away. Next he was presented with his building blocks, with which he happily played again, showing discrimination or the ability to differentiate among stimuli. Albert then allowed the rat to crawl towards him, while he kept completely still. When the rat touched Albert's hand, he withdrew it immediately. Watson and Rayner then placed the rat on his arm and Albert began to fret. They let the rat crawl across his chest and he covered his eyes with both hands. Albert's reaction to the presentation of the rabbit was very muted at first. But after a few seconds he tried to push it away with his feet. However, as the rabbit came nearer, he reached out to touch its ear; when it was placed in his lap, however, he started to cry and, at one point, characteristically sought comfort through thumb-sucking. When presented with the dog, Albert began to cry and covered his face with his hands. Watson and Rayner concluded that these experiments 'would seem to show conclusively that directly conditioned emotional responses as well as those conditioned by transfer persist, although with a certain loss in the intensity of the reaction, for a longer period than one month'.[7]

Watson and Rayner were also planning to test the removal of the conditioned emotional responses from Albert, but this proved impossible since they report that, 'unfortunately Albert was taken from the hospital the day before tests were made'.[8] They concluded that the emotional responses they had conditioned in Albert would persist indefinitely unless an accidental method for removing them was encountered. Nevertheless, Watson and Rayner outlined how they would have attempted to remove Albert's conditioned responses. They suggested that they would have constantly presented the conditioned stimulus (the rat) without the presentation of the unconditioned stimulus (the sound) and that, with repeated trials, the child would have habituated to the stimuli.

Alternatively, they would have tried a form of 're-conditioning' whereby they might have paired pleasurable sensations with the fear-inducing stimuli. They suggested these might have included feeding Albert sweets just as the rat was presented or 'simultaneously stimulating the erogenous zones (by touch) ... first the lips, then the nipples and as a final resort the sex organs'.[9]

In their original 1920 report, Watson and Rayner added further observations about the study. They discussed the fact that when emotionally upset Albert would often resort to thumb-sucking as a form of comfort. They noted that while doing this Albert was impervious to the fear-producing stimulus. To stop this happening, the researchers had had continually to pull his thumb out of his mouth.

The lessons from Little Albert

So what can we make of this case study? Did Watson and Rayner manage to demonstrate the acquisition of a phobia (an exaggerated, illogical fear of an object or category of objects) through classical conditioning? Should it be cited as a piece of classic, groundbreaking research into the effects of classical conditioning on behaviour or are there justifiable areas of concern regarding the ethical treatment of the participant, as well as further methodological criticisms that cannot be ignored?

One problem with the Little Albert study is that so many discrepancies and myths have evolved from it. Indeed, it has been claimed that 'most accounts of Watson and Rayner's research with Albert feature as much fabrication and distortion as they do fact. From information about Albert himself to the basic experimental methods and results, no detail of the original study has escaped misrepresentation in the telling and retelling of this bit of social science folklore.'[10]

It has been demonstrated that numerous textbooks have made serious mistakes about the exact details reported in the original 1920 article. This is attributed to many factors. The most likely source of confusion, and perhaps the most surprising, is Watson himself. Watson wrote a number of articles in subsequent years detailing the Albert case study and often seems to have (mis)reported various important details that do not concur with the original.[11] For example, Watson subsequently failed to mention that he and Rayner had been aware that Albert would be leaving the hospital and that they knew the reconditioning of Albert would thus become impossible. Did Watson deliberately omit this important detail in order to make the study appear less heartless?

Examples of textbook errors include conditioning of different stimuli such as a man's beard, a cat and a teddy bear. Many texts change the ending to report that Watson and Rayner did remove (or re-condition) Albert's fear. Possible reasons for such errors are the desire to tell ethically pleasing stories and/or to make the evidence 'fit in' with everyday explanations of how organisms act – in essence, to make the findings more readily believable. It is also thought that such changes help portray the study, and Watson's role in it, in a far more favourable light. Any criticisms of the study would be seen as a criticism of both behaviourism and its leading and most influential exponent.

So are these errors just slips of the pen or are they more serious than that? On closer inspection, there are also a number of serious methodological criticisms that can be made of the original 1920 study: Watson and Rayner's procedure of removing Albert's thumb from his mouth on various occasions in order to obtain the fear response; Albert being forced occasionally to touch some (but not all) of the stimuli; and the decision periodically to 'freshen up the [fear] reaction a bit'. These actions suggest that the experimental procedures were not standardised. The lack of detail regarding such behaviours brings into question the precise experimental techniques used. These are serious criticisms of the research and particularly ironic given Watson's emphasis on objective, scientific methods. Another problem with the Little Albert study is that subsequent researchers have been unable to replicate it – surely a prerequisite of science and a further indication that 'the [conditioning] process is not as simple as the story of Albert suggests'.[12]

Why did Watson not replicate his Albert study with other infants? Indeed, Watson had spent his earlier career testing animals and had never previously relied on a single participant. Many books suggest that Watson was unable to do this because he resigned his position at Johns Hopkins University very soon after the original study. Again, such stories may reflect a desire to make the account more believable since, in fact, Watson did actually continue at the university until September 1920, well over six months after the Albert study was published. In addition, Watson continued to play an active part in behavioural research projects for many years to come and would certainly have had the opportunity to supervise a direct replication of the study.

There is also some question as to exactly how much of a fear reaction was induced in Little Albert.[13] It has been suggested that Albert did not develop a phobia to rats nor even a consistent or pronounced fear of them or any other animals. Even in the original paper, the description of Albert's reaction to the rat after eight conditioning trials over a ten-day period revealed that although he did try to crawl away, 'there was no crying, but strange to say, as he started away he began to gurgle and coo'. There are further descriptions such as 'fear reaction slight ... allowed the rat to crawl towards him without withdrawing', 'reached out tentatively and slowly and touched the rabbit's ear with his right hand, finally manipulating it'. All of these responses seem at odds with the strength of feeling one would normally associate with a marked fear or phobia. How many people with a spider phobia would willingly reach out and touch one?

Given all these inconsistencies it is no surprise that the study 'could not have become enshrined as the paradigm for human conditioning on the basis of its hard scientific evidence'.[14] Even Watson himself described the study as being

> in such an incomplete state that the verified conclusions are not possible; hence this summary, like so many other bits of psychological work, must be looked upon merely as a preliminary exposition of possibilities rather than a catalogue of concrete usable results.[15]

This quote is in direct contrast to the one mentioned above, where Watson and Rayner describe the Albert study as 'as convincing a case of a completely conditioned fear response as could have been theoretically pictured'. So which version are we to believe, and why has this study become such a 'classic'?

Academic debate

At the end of their journal article, Watson and Rayner ridiculed the Freudian analyst who might one day find him/herself treating Albert's phobia. They stated:

> The Freudians twenty years from now, unless their hypotheses change, when they come to analyze Albert's fear of a seal skin coat — assuming that he comes to analysis at that age – will probably tease from him the recital of a dream which upon their analysis will show that Albert at three years of age attempted to play with the pubic hair of the mother and was scolded violently for it. (We are by no means denying that this might in some other case condition it.) If the analyst has sufficiently prepared Albert to accept such a dream when found as an explanation of his avoiding tendencies, and if the analyst has the authority and personality to put it over, Albert may be fully convinced that the dream was a true revealer of the factors which brought about the fear.[16]

The inclusion of this paragraph suggests two things. First, it confirms that Watson and Rayner believed that Albert's phobia might persist into adulthood; second, it suggests a rather uncaring or flippant attitude towards this state of affairs. Whatever one's opinion of Freudian interpretations, it seems incredible that Watson and Rayner felt they could use Albert's misfortune (brought about entirely by their own actions) to poke fun at Freudian therapists' views of phobic acquisition.

Ethical issues

Watson and Rayner's research would never be allowed to go ahead under the ethical guidelines we have in place today. Some people might argue that it is unfair to impose current ethical standards on a piece of research that is over 80 years old. Indeed, the ethics of the techniques used by Watson and Rayner did not seem to attract open criticism at the time,[17] and this cultural change is an interesting subject in itself. In 1920, psychologists did not have a set of written ethical guidelines to follow. There is little doubt that at least one of today's key ethical rules – namely, protection of the participant from both psychological and physical harm – was broken. Albert certainly appeared to suffer a great deal of distress and this may have continued beyond the duration of the study. Watson and Rayner wrote that it was unfortunate that Albert was removed from the hospital before they had a chance to re-condition him. As mentioned above, their subsequent writings hint that they were taken by surprise at his departure, but a closer reading of the original report makes clear that they knew of his departure a month in advance. In any case, exactly how difficult would it have been to locate Albert at a later date and offer his mother the chance for them to re-condition him? The question of how hard they tried to minimise any permanent harm suffered by Albert remains unanswered. Watson and Rayner discussed the possibility of harm being caused, but stated that they decided to go ahead in the belief that many of the conditioned emotional reactions they were planning might have been acquired by Albert in his everyday life, in 'the rough and tumble of the home'. This may have satisfied both Watson and Rayner, but it is surely questionable as to how many of the reactions might have been encountered. Many children may well encounter rabbits, but not usually at the same time as an unexpected and unpleasant noise sounds behind their head. Indeed, most children probably have very positive initial encounters with rabbits and dogs. These positive associations lead many of them, from an early age, to want to keep their own pets. Although it is clear that a small minority of children do, through particular circumstances, naturally develop phobias – of dogs, say – this does not justify the deliberate infliction of one.

It may be that it was fortunate for Albert that Watson and Rayner did not manage to 're-condition' him, since the techniques they suggested they might have used to do this seem dubious in the extreme. It is often reported that they were planning to re-condition him by pairing the rat (by now the conditioned stimulus) with a pleasurable stimulus, such as sweets, to try to reverse the effects of the unpleasant noise association. They also suggested, however, as we have already seen, that they would have used other methods too, including tactual stimulation of the lips, then the nipples and, as a last resort, the sex organs. This is far less readily reported, yet today these outrageous methods would surely be regarded as a form of child sexual abuse.

Further studies: Little Peter

Watson did, indeed, supervise and advise on further studies that involved young children and their fears and phobias. These experiments, although supervised by Watson, were actually conducted by Mary Cover Jones.[18] The goal of the research was systematically to study the best method for the elimination of children's fears. Children (aged from three months to seven years) from a local care home, who already had a fear of certain situations such as the dark, sudden presentation of a rat, a rabbit, a frog, and so on, were the participants. Jones tried many different methods of elimination including, finally, direct conditioning.

The child in Jones's 'direct conditioning' case was named 'Peter'.[19] The case of 'Little Peter' is widely recognised as the sequel to the Little Albert case study, and gave Watson and Jones the chance to test the principles of 're-conditioning' that they had not implemented with Albert. Peter was two years ten months old and intensely afraid of various things, including rats, rabbits, fur coats and cotton wool. Initially, they tried to lessen his fears using 'modelling' techniques whereby he was allowed to observe and interact with children who played happily with a white rabbit – one of his feared objects. The rabbit was moved closer to Peter each day and this 'gradual' technique seemed to have a positive effect to the extent that he could eventually pat the rabbit on the back. Unfortunately, Peter then contracted scarlet fever and during the ensuing two-month delay was scared by a large dog. This event, Watson and Jones reported, meant that his fears of various animals, including the rabbit, reoccurred. A new technique was devised. This involved presenting food (an unconditioned pleasant stimulus) simultaneously with the rabbit (the conditioned stimulus). The rabbit was gradually brought closer to Peter, in conjunction with his favourite food. Peter grew more and more tolerant of the rabbit (presumably associating it with his liking for the food) and was able to touch the rabbit without fear. When his fears spontaneously returned the researchers used a similar counter-conditioning method where he was allowed to play while the rabbit was gradually brought closer and closer to him over a series of sessions. Eventually Peter was able to play happily with the rabbit. This is thought to be the first case of behavioural therapy and laid the foundation for Joseph Wolpe's later work into systematic desensitisation. Although Wolpe[20] is generally credited with developing the technique, he acknowledged his debt to Mary Cover Jones. As a result of the Little Peter study and her subsequent research, Jones gained the informal title 'the mother of behavioural therapy'.

What happened to Little Albert and Watson?

There is no record of what happened to Little Albert, or whether his fears persisted into adulthood or were extinguished over time, perhaps due to habituation or through some form of counter-conditioning. We can be more certain of what happened to J.B. Watson. During the Little Albert study, he was having an extra-marital affair with his co-author Rosalie Rayner. The scandal that ensued when this became public knowledge meant that he was subsequently forced to resign his academic appointment just as his ideas were gaining more acceptance in the wider scientific community. There may have been no set of ethical guidelines to protect research participants like Albert in the 1920s but there were strict moral standards that academics were expected to follow. Bitterly disappointed, Watson took his knowledge of psychology and human behaviour and applied it in the far more financially lucrative area of advertising. He pioneered the use of classical conditioning techniques in advertising campaigns. Watson was convinced that successful advertising was not entirely dependent on the quality of the product but on the emotional responses that consumers would associate with each product. To this end he exhorted advertisers to 'tell him something that will tie him up with fear, something that will stir up a mild rage, that will call out an affectionate or love response, or strike at a deep psychological or habit need'.[21]

Nowadays, thanks in no small part to Watson, classical conditioning is used in a glut of advertisements. The idea is to produce an advert (the unconditioned stimulus) and make sure that it elicits a positive response (unconditioned response) in the viewing public. The product being advertised thus becomes the conditioned stimulus. The next time someone is shopping they associate the positive feeling they had for the advert with the product. The positive feeling they have for the product is now the conditioned response, and the advertisers hope this will lead them to purchase the product in order to prolong the response.

Using such techniques, Watson helped shape creative advertising campaigns for, among others, Maxwell House Coffee, Pond's Cold Cream, Johnson's Baby Powder, Odorono (one of the first deodorants) and Pebeco Toothpaste. In the baby powder advertisements he played on the fears that young mothers have in relation to looking after their children. In the Pebeco Toothpaste campaign, he associated the brand with sexually arousing cues. A seductively dressed young woman was pictured smoking a cigarette, with the words 'You can smoke and still be lovely if you'll just use Pebeco twice a day.' Here the attractive woman was the unconditioned stimulus and the toothpaste the conditioned stimulus. It has been claimed that Watson was the man who put the 'sex' into the phrase 'sex sells'.

Watson also placed a great deal of emphasis on empirical marketing research by stressing the importance of knowing the consumer through scientific study. He viewed the process of selling as a laboratory for advertising and made frequent comparisons between the consumer and experimental participants. In the same way that he had manipulated Albert's behaviour, he believed that, with the appropriate reinforcers, advertisers could manipulate consumers' buying behaviour. To this end, Watson developed marketing research techniques and was one of the first to study the idea of brand loyalty – a subject studied by advertisers to this day.

Watson's success in advertising ensured that by 1924 he had become vice president of the J. Walter Thompson (JWT) advertising agency – one of the largest ad agencies in the world. His personal life was less successful, however. Soon after divorcing his first wife, he married Rosalie Rayner. Their marriage produced two children but, unfortunately, Rosalie died of complications due to dysentery, aged just 35. Watson retired from advertising in 1945 and burnt all his unpublished works shortly before his death in 1958.

One of the most memorable (and most cited) quotes from Watson put forward the case for environmental influences on behaviour:

> Give me a dozen healthy infants, well-formed, and my own specified world to bring them up and I'll guarantee to take any one at random and train him to become any type of specialist I might select – doctor, lawyer, merchant-chief, and yes, even beggarman and thief, regardless of his talents, penchants, tendencies, abilities, vocations, and race of his ancestors.[22]

But the sentence that follows is cited less often. He added, 'I'm going beyond my facts and I admit it, but so have advocates of the contrary and they have been doing it for thousands of years.'

One of the lessons to be learned from the Little Albert case study is to do with the way that (questionable) experimental evidence can inadvertently be misinterpreted and re-evaluated. These second-hand myths get taken as 'facts' and they, in their turn, help confer a study with the status of a 'classic'. There is no doubt that the case study of Little Albert remains a 'classic' in psychology, but the question remains as to whether it deserves its place on the basis of its experimental findings alone. Perhaps it deserves its status on the basis of the influence (deserved or otherwise) it had on thinking at the time, an influence that continues to this day.

1. Watson, J.B. and Rayner, R. (1920) Conditioned emotional reactions. *Journal of Experimental Psychology* 3(1), pp. 1–14.
2. Watson and Rayner, Conditioned emotional reactions, p. 2.
3. Ibid.
4. Ibid.
5. Ibid.
6. The most famous of behaviourist psychologists, B.F. Skinner, called this type of learning 'respondent conditioning' because it involves a response to an environmental antecedent.
7. Watson and Rayner, Conditioned emotional reactions, p. 6.
8. Ibid.
9. Ibid.
10. Harris, B. (1979) Whatever happened to Little Albert? *American Psychologist* 34(2), pp. 151–60.
11. Watson, J.B. and Watson, R.R. (1921) Studies in infant psychology. *Scientific Monthly* 13, pp. 493–515.
12. Hilgard, E. and Maquis, D. (1940) *Conditioning and Learning*. New York: Appleton-Century, p. 293.
13. Harris, Whatever happened, pp. 151–60.
14. Samuelson, F. (1980) J.B. Watson's Little Albert, Cyril Burt's Twins and the need for a critical science. *American Psychologist* 35(7), pp. 619–25 (this quote, p. 621).
15. Watson and Watson, Studies in infant psychology, pp. 493–515.
16. Watson and Rayner, Conditioned emotional reactions, p. 7.
17. Gross, R.D. (2003) *Key Studies in Psychology* (4th edn). London: Hodder & Stoughton, p. 311.
18. Jones, M.C. (1924) Elimination of children's fears. *Journal of Experimental Psychology* 7, pp. 381–90.
19. Jones, M.C. (1924) A laboratory study of fear: the case of Peter. *Pedagogical Seminary* 31, pp. 308–15.
20. Wolpe, J. (1958) *Psychotherapy by Reciprocal Inhibition*. Stanford, Conn.: Stanford University Press.
21. Buckley, K.W. (1982) The selling of a psychologist: John Broadus Watson and the application of behavioral techniques to advertising. *Journal of the History of the Behavioral Sciences* 18, pp. 207–21.
22. Watson, J.B. (1924) *Behaviorism*. Chicago, Ill.: University of Chicago Press, p. 82.

14 | The man with no brain?

Professor John Lorber looked at the brain scan of the student in front of him. The student was studying for a maths degree and had a recorded IQ of 126 (100 is the average person's score). The student had been referred to Lorber by the university campus doctor, who had noticed that his head was slightly larger than normal. Knowing Lorber's research interests into hydrocephalus[1] he thought the student might be worthy of further investigation. The brain scan showed that the student had practically no brain at all. It was estimated that his brain would have weighed no more than 150 grams; the normal brain weight for a man of his age would be 1.5 kilograms. This, combined with further very rare cases, led Lorber and others to pose the question 'Is the brain really necessary?' This has cast doubt on our understanding of the workings of the human brain, and has been cited as evidence in perpetuating the widely held belief that we use only 10 per cent of our brains.

Background

The human brain is the most complex organ known to man. It has about 100,000,000,000 (100 billion) neurons and there are 1000 to 10,000 synapses (connections) for *each* of these neurons. These synapses can transmit about ten impulses per second, which works out at a maximum limit of 10 quadrillion synapse operations per second! These numbers are hard to take in, but somebody has worked out that a pile of 100 billion pieces of paper would be about 5000 miles high – the distance from San Francisco to London.[2] The average human brain accounts for about 2 per cent of body weight, but greedily consumes about 25 per cent of the body's energy.

Given such facts and figures, it is unsurprising that much is still unknown about the human brain. Physiologists and psychologists have spent years trying to locate the areas of the brain responsible for different functions. The early science of phrenology (see Chapter 10), which originated in the theories of a Viennese physician called Franz Joseph Gall, tried to address this. Gall believed that the shape of the brain was determined by the development of its constituent organs and, since the skull takes its shape from the brain, the surface of the skull should offer clues to a person's psychological abilities and personality; for example, a bump located on the forehead might indicate a person's kindness. Despite having enjoyed great popularity in the Victorian era (in the 1830s, some employers even used to demand a character reference from a phrenologist as part of vetting prospective job applicants!) phrenology had been almost completely discredited by the mid-nineteenth century.[3]

However, one of the assumptions behind phrenology – namely 'brain localisation of function' – persists to this day. Localisation of function simply means that different parts of the brain carry out different functions (vision, voluntary movement, language, and so on). Although this may seem obvious, some other internal organs, such as the liver, do not function in this way – that is, all parts of the liver essentially perform the same task. It took years of further clinical research evidence to discover that the phrenologists' assumption regarding the localisation of function in the brain, if not the precise details surrounding it, had been right all along.

Early research

One of the early pioneers to turn to these more scientific ways of studying the brain was Karl Lashley (1890–1958). Lashley hoped to find the location of memory traces, or engrams, in the brain. Working with rats, he trained them to learn to run through mazes. Then he systematically removed (lesioned) portions (up to 50 per cent) of their cerebral cortex to see the effects. Lashley found that large portions of the cortex could be removed without apparently affecting the rats' memories.[4] Lashley used to joke that locating the engram wasn't a problem, but finding where it *wasn't* was! As a result of such work, Lashley formulated two principles. First, that all areas of the cerebral cortex are important in learning and memory, and that one cortical area can substitute for another (this he called the equipotentiality principle) and, second, that memories for complex tasks are stored throughout the cerebral cortex (the principle of mass action) and are not isolated in any particular area. In essence, the strength of the memory depends on the amount of tissue available. The location of the lesion was not as vital as the amount of tissue destroyed.

The idea of rats with very little cerebral cortex still being able to recall their way through mazes led some people to question whether the cortex was a vital component in learning at all. Findings from studies including Lashley's were misinterpreted and it soon became a widespread belief that humans use only 10 per cent of their brains.

Other research involving experiments and case studies had found that there were, indeed, very specific areas of the brain responsible for different functions (Broca's area, for instance, controls speech production). Lashley's testing methods were simply not sophisticated enough to uncover the source of memory. Nevertheless, he was correct to hint that much learning involves wide parallel interconnections of neurons distributed throughout the brain. Such a process gives the appearance of 'mass action' (the brain operating as a single organism), but has been more accurately compared to a symphony orchestra with many separate sections (violins, percussion, and so on) contributing to the finished, coherent piece.

Despite increasing research evidence to the contrary, the public debate regarding the role of the cerebral cortex continued. For instance, although not documented, it is widely reported that Einstein once joked that his intelligence was the result of tapping into the unused areas of his brain.

The man with no brain

John Lorber, a paediatrician and acknowledged expert on spina bifida was thrust into this debate after examining a patient referred to him by a GP working on the campus of Sheffield University. Lorber was a surgeon who specialised in the treatment of hydrocephalus. Hydrocephalus comes from the Greek words 'hydro', which means water, and 'cephalus', which means head. Hydrocephalus involves an abnormally large accumulation of cerebrospinal fluid (CSF) within the cavities (ventricles) inside the brain. If the CSF is not absorbed quickly enough, it builds up pressure in the ventricles and this causes the cerebral cortex to be crushed outwards against the skull. Lorber was performing surgery on people with hydrocephalus by inserting valves called 'shunts' in order to relieve the pressure caused by the build-up of CSF. He was surprised by a few patients who seemed to have few or no mental deficits but who, on brain scans, were seen to have such extremely enlarged ventricles that there was virtually no discernible cerebral cortex at all.

His best-known case involved a maths undergraduate with an IQ of 126, who subsequently went on to gain a first-class honours degree. Lorber claimed that his cerebral cortex, as shown on the scan, was a mere millimetre or so thick (crushed by the effects of hydrocephalus) compared to the usual four or five centimetres. Lorber reckoned that his whole brain weighed a mere 150 grams compared to the typical 1500 grams. Lorber subsequently published a paper with the provocative title 'Is your brain really necessary?',[5] questioning the need for some areas of the cerebral cortex. On a subsequent television documentary he stated, 'My hunch is that we all have a substantial reserve of neurons and brain cells … that we don't need and don't use'.[6] Lorber claimed to have documented about 600 such cases and categorised them into four groups. These were (i) those cases with near normal brains, (ii) and those with 50–70 per cent, (iii) 70–90 per cent and (iv) 95 per cent of the cranium filled with CSF. There were only about 60 cases in this last group and approximately half of these were profoundly retarded. The other half, which included the maths graduate, had IQs above 100. In the past, in children whose skulls had not yet calcified, the cranium would often balloon outwards due to internal pressure. Before the modern technique of 'shunts' was used, such an affliction was likely to lead to death. So do such case studies suggest that much of the cerebral cortex is redundant or are there alternative explanations?

Conflicting evidence

The first point to be made is that in many of these cases there may have been some exaggeration of the extent of brain loss. Lorber used a CAT (computerised axial tomography) scan technique to view the internal structure of the brain. This is an X-ray procedure that, when combined with a computer, can generate cross-sectional views of the internal organs and structures of the body. It is suggested that a cerebral cortex of only a millimetre or so thick would probably not have shown up clearly on such a scan, meaning that in reality the cortex might have been somewhat larger. Lorber conceded that the reading of CAT scans is difficult, but remained convinced that his interpretation of the evidence was correct. More advanced brain-scanning techniques have shown that the cerebral cortex is not 'lost' or destroyed, but compacted into the smaller space available. If anything, this demonstrates the remarkable ability of the brain to adapt to circumstances. This is also supported by studies of neural damage in infants. It is well documented that children can more readily adapt to serious head injuries than adults due to the plasticity and adaptability of their brains. There are cases of children who have had one brain hemisphere surgically removed regaining, after a period of some adjustment, most of their former abilities, including language. This suggests that the remaining areas of the brain have taken over the functions of the removed hemisphere. This 'crowding' procedure may also have occurred in the case of the maths graduate reported by Lorber.

There have also been question marks over the lack of deficit reported in some of Lorber's patients, most notably the maths graduate. Some of the effects of hydrocephalus are quite subtle and are not readily detectable on standard cognition tests such as IQ.

How necessary is the brain?

Despite the Lorber case study, it appears that the cerebral cortex is essential. There are well-documented cases of people suffering extreme cognitive deficits after fairly minor neurological damage. If much of our grey matter were redundant then it would be expected that people could cope quite easily after brain trauma. In addition, it seems unlikely that natural selection would have resulted in an organ that consumes so much energy for so little return. Other costs of having a large brain concern the risks to mother and child during childbirth. A smaller, more efficient brain that could cope with the same cognitive functions would surely have been advantageous and therefore naturally selected. The fact that we do have a large brain suggests some sort of selective advantage. Redundancy is fine if there are no costs, but here the costs of having a large brain seem to outweigh the benefits of a small, but more efficient, brain.

Modern brain-scanning techniques have also shown how much of the brain is used in different activities. They demonstrate that large areas of the brain are used in almost all activities. Even during sleep, that seemingly most passive of activities, the brain is surprisingly active, particularly when we are dreaming. So much so that dream sleep is often referred to as 'active sleep'.

Before his death in 1996, Lorber, who had a reputation for being deliberately controversial, conceded that he had perhaps over-dramatised his evidence, arguing that this needed to be done in order to get people to listen. He believed that far too often results that don't fit existing explanations are marginalised as 'anomalous'. Lorber continued to argue that there must be some redundancy or spare capacity in the brain, in much the same way that there is in the kidney or liver. There is some further experimental evidence of rats to support Lorber's claims. Rats that have large areas of the cerebral cortex removed in one go seem to suffer from gross dysfunction, but rats that have the same amount of cortex removed in a series of stages can cope remarkably well and show little sign of impairment. This appears to mirror the gradual step-by-step effects of hydrocephalus seen in some of Lorber's patients. To this day, the idea of spare capacity in the brain remains a controversial and contentious argument, but it seems most likely that reallocation of function *is* possible, particularly in the developing child's brain.

Given the evidence, it is certain that the cerebral cortex is necessary and that the claim that we use only 10 per cent of our brain is nothing more than a myth or 'urban legend'. We can be fairly certain that we use our entire brain all the time. The Lorber case study provides a fascinating peek into the workings of the brain, but rather than offering evidence of its redundancy it provides further evidence of its amazing adaptability and complexity – a complexity we are only just beginning to comprehend.

1. Hydrocephalus is a condition, often congenital, in which an abnormal accumulation of fluid in the cerebral ventricles causes enlargement of the skull and compression of the brain, destroying neurons in the process.
2. Source: www.brainconnection.com.
3. Source: http://pages.britishlibrary.net/phrenology/overview.htm#whatwasit.
4. Lashley, K. (1950) In search of the engram, in *Physiological Mechanisms in Animal Behaviour*. New York: Academic Press, pp. 454–82.
5. Lorber, J. (1981) Is your brain really necessary? *Nursing Mirror* 152, pp. 29–30.
6. Reported in an excellent article by Beyerstein, B. (1998) Whence cometh the myth that we only use ten per cent of our brains? A later version of this article was published in Della Sala, S. (1999) *Mind-Myths*. Chichester: John Wiley & Sons.

15 Freud's analysis of phobia in a young boy: the story of Little Hans

Sigmund Freud is the best-known psychologist of all time. He produced a whole body of work covering a diverse range of topics, from child and personality development to the meaning of dreams, as well as the therapeutic treatment of mental disorders. Freud primarily used the case study method for his research. Although he mentions as many as 133 cases in his writings he documents only six detailed accounts of individuals. Such was Freud's influence that some of his patients subsequently became minor celebrities of their time. Despite his emphasis on the importance of childhood experiences to adult development, Freud documented only one case study of a child. For this reason the case study of Little Hans is of crucial importance in Freudian theory. This landmark study of child analysis caused great excitement and controversy when first published and continues to do so to this day.

Friendship with Freud

In his day, Max Graf (1873–1958) was a well-known author, critic and acknowledged scholar on the history, theory and science of music. Nowadays, he is perhaps more famous as a good friend of Sigmund Freud (1856–1939). He holds a unique position in the annals of psychoanalysis since he was also the father of 'Little Hans'.

Graf met Freud because his wife was one of the analyst's early patients. Indeed, she was a patient of Freud's before she and Graf were married, and it's reported that Freud encouraged their union. The couple used to attend a Wednesday-night study group at Freud's home at 19 Berggasse, Vienna. Other notable members of the group included Alfred Adler and Carl Jung. These members might be regarded as Freud's early 'disciples', and the group later evolved into the Vienna Psychoanalytic Society. Freud hoped that psychoanalysis might break through disciplinary boundaries, so people like Max Graf, who came from the field of art, were particularly welcome. Graf was obviously a huge admirer of Freud and later described him as the most cultivated person he knew.

Freud encouraged his group members to collect developmental data on their own children and the Grafs proved to be particularly diligent at this. They started to keep detailed notes on their son's early years. Max Graf took this a stage further and, under Freud's guidance, attempted the first analysis of his own son. Throughout this period of analysis, Max Graf consulted Freud, and Freud closely monitored and advised on the therapeutic process. This process was subsequently reported by Freud in 1909 in a paper entitled 'The analysis of a phobia in a five-year-old boy'.[1] The five-year-old was given the pseudonym 'Hans'.

Freud had already written an account of the theory of childhood sexuality, published in 1905,[2] and intended to use the Little Hans case study as a test of this theory. His theory of sexuality had not been well received in many quarters and had variously been described as abominably immoral and obscene. In addition, Freud set out to detail the development and resolution of a phobia as a form of neurotic disorder.

Freud mentioned Hans briefly in earlier writings. For example, in a 1907 article on sexuality he referred to a three-year-old boy who guessed the truth about birth, having seen his mother pregnant. In these articles, Hans is referred to by his real name, Herbert. It is believed that Freud decided to rename Herbert after a famous horse of the time nicknamed 'Clever Hans', who was reported to have been capable of simple mathematical tasks[3] such as counting (the horse used to tap his hoof to supply the correct number in 'answer' to a sum posed to him). Freud must have felt that the name was appropriate given Herbert's phobia of horses and the fact that he was such an intelligent boy.

'Little Hans'

'Little Hans' was born in Vienna on 10 April 1903. He was described as a cheerful, straightforward child who had a loving upbringing in a typical middle-class family. He was happy and talkative, and loved both his mother and father. The Grafs were close friends of Freud's. Close enough for Freud to give Hans a generous birthday present. Surprisingly, given their son's horse phobia, Freud chose as a gift a rocking horse. In 1942, Max Graf claimed this was given on Hans's third birthday, but ten years later he referred to it as his son's fifth-birthday present.[4] If it was a gift for his third birthday, it was a remarkable coincidence that he would later develop a horse phobia, so it seems more likely that Freud gave it to him on his fifth birthday as a convincing (and amusing) demonstration that his phobia had been cured. Incidentally, the occasion of the giving of the present was only the second time that Freud had met Hans; previously, they had met in a short therapeutic session. They did not meet again until many years later when Hans was an adult.

The close relationship Max Graf had with Freud is demonstrated by the fact that he discussed with Freud the possibility of raising Herbert as a Catholic rather than a Jew. Graf had experienced at first hand the hatred towards Jews in Vienna at the beginning of the twentieth century and sought advice from Freud as to the best course of action to protect his young son. Although no doubt recognising the inherent dangers, Freud suggested that being brought up as a Jew subjected to discrimination would help foster an inner dynamism in Herbert that would be useful in later life; thus he remained Jewish.

So what techniques did Freud use in his study of Hans? As mentioned, he used the case study method and followed Hans (primarily using second-hand accounts from Max Graf) from the age of three to five years (1906–1908). The data collected included biographical information and shorthand notes exclusively reported by Hans's parents. Max Graf also used to consult with Freud directly about his son. There was only one occasion when Freud played a direct part in the treatment of Hans and that was a conversation that took place on 30 March 1908 when the boy's analysis was coming to an end. The analytical techniques used included analyses of fantasies, Hans's general behaviour and his phobias, as well as dream analysis. Freud believed that the interpretation of dreams was the 'royal road' to the understanding of the unconscious. For Freud, each dream has a manifest and latent content. The manifest part is that which can be recalled, whereas the latent part is hidden. It is in the latent part where the real meaning of the dream might be uncovered.

The analysis of phobia in a young boy

The 'Little Hans' case study is detailed and complicated. Freud's writings about Little Hans, when translated into English, occupy about 150 pages. However, apart from the original, there are numerous readable accounts of the details of the case.[5] The psychoanalytic interpretation of events is often surprising and contentious. Freud's angle on the significant events of Hans's formative years can be summarised as follows.

He reports Hans showing 'a quite peculiarly lively interest in his "widdler" [penis]'. Hans used to enjoy touching his own penis and, to try to stop this, one day his mother threatened to cut it off. Despite his castration anxiety, his pleasure in this sexual activity widened. For example, he observed that animals at the local zoo had 'widdlers' that were correspondingly much larger than his own; he also expressed regret that he had seen neither his father's nor his mother's 'widdlers'. He assumed that, since they were grown up, their 'widdlers' would also be large 'like a horse'.

During one summer holiday, Hans's father was absent for long periods of time and Hans realised that he liked having his mother to himself. At first, Hans wished his father would 'go away', but later he wished he would go away per-manently – that is, die. The event that Freud supposed most influenced Hans's psychosexual development was the birth of his little sister, Hannah, when he was three and a half years old. The birth caused Hans great anxiety and he felt hostility towards his sister, afraid that she would occupy too much of his mother's time. He expressed this anxiety indirectly in a fear of taking a bath, thinking that his mother might drop him in the bath but, in reality, hoping that she might drop his sister. In analysis, Hans gave undisguised expression to the death wish he had against his sister, but didn't consider this as as wicked as the one he had against his father.

One day, while in the street, Hans had an anxiety attack. Although he could not say what he was afraid of, it appeared that his motive for being ill was the chance to stay at home and cuddle more with his mother. In time, his fear heightened to the extent that he was afraid even when his mother accompanied him. Hans also reported a quite specific fear that a white horse would bite him. Today this might sound rather a peculiar thing to be afraid of, but the Vienna that Hans knew would have had working horses everywhere, transporting peo-ple and all manner of goods throughout the city.

There were two dimensions to Hans's phobia about horses. He had once heard a father warning his child, on leaving a horse-drawn carriage, 'Don't put your finger to the white horse or it'll bite you.' Freud guessed that the first half of this sentence echoed the wording his mother had used to warn Hans about touching his 'widdler'. In addition, Hans had been informed by his father that women do not have penises and made the connection with the castration threat from his mother earlier, reasoning that she must have had her penis cut off. Thus the connection between Hans's castration anxiety and horses was made.

Hans next reported a fantasy about two giraffes. He said he had had a dream about taking away a crumpled giraffe (representing his mother), and a big giraffe protesting and crying out (representing his father). Freud informed Hans that he was afraid of his father because of his hostile thoughts towards him. Freud also interpreted Hans's fear of horses, suggesting that the horse must rep-resent his father: the black skin round a white horse's mouth, and its blinkers, were said to represent his father's moustache and glasses. After the meeting with Freud, Max recorded a conversation where Hans said, 'Daddy don't trot away from me!'

Hans gave further details of his phobia (which he referred to as his 'non-sense'). He reported being afraid of horses falling down, and frightened of heav-ily loaded carts, vans or buses. Hans also recalled an event where he saw a horse fall down in the street and kick about with its feet. He was terrified and thought the horse was dead. Hans's father pointed out that when he saw the horse dead he must have thought of him. Hans had displaced his fear of his father on to horses, which reminded him of his father. For Hans, this realisation, or explanation, appears to have been a turning point. Freud reported that Hans appeared to accept this theory and from then on was unconstrained and fearless in his relationship with his father.

Hans also gradually became less fearful of horses. Two concluding fantasies suggested that he had resolved his feelings about his father. In the first, Hans reported that a plumber came and took away his 'widdler' and then gave him another larger one. In the second, Hans told his father that he imagined himself as the father of his own imaginary children, not as their mother as had usually been the case. According to Freud, both fantasies showed that he had moved from wishing his father dead to identifying with him. With these two fantasies both Hans's illness and his analysis came to an end.

Freud's focus

One of the key themes of Freud's work is the importance of the first few years of life in the subsequent development of personality. He believed that children experience emotional conflicts, and their future wellbeing depends on how well these are resolved. Freud believed that, by communicating his fears, Hans had successfully resolved his conflicts and anxieties.

In contrast to the thinking of his day, Freud believed that children were usually sexual before puberty. He held that infantile sexuality shows up at different stages of development, with a focus at each stage on a different part of the body. Freud believed that the case study of Little Hans provided support for this concept. He argued that all children pass through five stages of development: the oral, anal, phallic, latent and genital. The first three stages occur during the child's first five years and it was the phallic stage that Hans had been passing through at the end of his analysis.

The phallic stage, from three to five years old, was, he thought, the stage where the child's sexual identification was established. During this stage Freud hypothesised that Hans, like all young boys, experienced what he called the Oedipus complex. This describes the desire of a child to possess sexually the opposite-sex parent (in this case Hans's mother) and to exclude the parent of the same sex (thus Hans's desire to exclude his father, Max Graf). Of course, Hans realised that the latter was impossible given the overwhelming power and strength of his father. According to Freud, Hans would have feared that his father might see him as a rival and castrate him. Such conflicts are, obviously,

disturbing to a child, and one way in which they seek to resolve them is to identify with the same-sex parent. According to Freud, Hans accomplished this by
developing a mechanism called 'identification with the aggressor'. This can be
seen in Hans's last fantasy, where he imagines himself as a father to his own
imaginary children. In this way, believed Freud, all young boys learn to identify
with their fathers. Freud proposed that girls experience the similar Electra complex, but his emphasis on male development has led to him being criticised as
sexist and 'phallocentric'.

Freud believed that the 'unconscious' is a part of the mind of which we are
not aware and that it contains a number of unresolved conflicts such as the
Oedipus complex. These conflicts affect our behaviour (hence Hans's phobia of
horses) and are revealed in our fantasies and dreams (the giraffe and plumber
fantasies). Due to their threatening or upsetting nature, the conflicts appear in
disguised form and need to be interpreted in order that their true significance
may be revealed.

Sigmund Fraud?

So what has the Little Hans case study contributed to the field of psychology?
Freud's supporters suggest that it demonstrates how some phobias develop in
children – simply as a means to cope with conflict and anxiety. Critics have put
forward alternative explanations, however. Perhaps one of the most plausible of
these is to do with the conditioned fear response through classical conditioning
(see also Chapter 13): the incident where Hans witnessed the horse collapsing in
the street was the actual cause of the disorder; the marked fear response to this
initial event generalised to all horses and a fear of going out in the street where
Hans would undoubtedly have encountered them.

Freud was the first to suggest that a so-called 'talking cure' would be appropriate in the case of a child as young as Hans. Throughout the case study, Freud
demonstrates his utmost respect for Hans's views. Indeed, at one point when
Hans is reprimanded by his father for wishing his sister drowned, Hans replies
that it is good to think it because it is evidence that might be useful for 'the
Professor [Freud]'. Freud reported that he could have wished for 'no better
understanding of psychoanalysis from any grown-up'. This incident might be
viewed as an example of 'demand characteristics', where a participant (Hans)
provides the answer that they think the researcher (Freud) would like to hear. As
such it can also be viewed as a criticism of Freud's techniques. Despite this, it is
far from preposterous to suggest that Freud's innovative and pioneering work
with Hans shaped the overall approach of much of the psychotherapeutic work

conducted with children today. Furthermore, Freud's assertions that the unconscious plays an important part in determining much of our behaviour is widely accepted today.

Analysis of the Little Hans case study has concentrated on the subjective reporting of the case. All of the reports were obtained either from Max Graf (Hans's father) or from Freud. There was no independent collaboration of the case. Hans's father was already a strong supporter of Freud's theories and may have presented the evidence accordingly. The special relationship that Hans had with his analyst father may make the case unique and mean that the results cannot be generalised. Freud was aware of these possible criticisms, but argued that the special relationship between Hans and his father was one of the reasons why the analysis was so successful. Freud argued that their relationship was a strength of the therapy, not a weakness, and that all psychoanalysts should aim to foster strong relationships with their clients.

From its advent to the present day, psychoanalysis has remained controversial. Given the evidence and interpretations placed on the case by both Max Graf and Freud, it is no surprise that the Little Hans case study is regarded by some as the most farcical case history on record. Psychoanalysis has been claimed to be 'a scientific fairytale' and totally ineffective as a therapy beyond its placebo effect. Psychoanalysis has even been compared to a cult, with Sigmund Freud as its high priest. Articles have been written promising to 'bury Freud'[6] and he has been denounced as a liar and a sexist. As the author of the 'seduction hypothesis' he has been held responsible for the misery of parents wrongly accused by their 'abused' children, and in his subsequent renunciation of the hypothesis he has been held responsible for the abuse of children.[7] People have wondered how such a flawed theory of the mind could have had such a marked influence on psychiatry for over half a century. They have questioned the way in which Freud's specious ideas, based on unconvincing evidence, have influenced psychiatry and society in general (for example, in the use of Freudian terminology), and this has been viewed as one of the most extraordinary events in the history of intellectual thinking in the twentieth century.

However, psychoanalysis has continued to develop since its Freudian beginnings. Freud was a product of his time and should surely be viewed as such. His approach to the inner workings of the human mind was revolutionary for its day. It may not pass muster in comparison to the scientific methods employed today, but compared well with contemporary methods. Freud was a trained scientist and regarded himself as an 'archaeologist of the mind', digging deeper and deeper into the unconscious. From his early days experimenting with cocaine, hypnosis and electrotherapy (all later abandoned) Freud had an intense, single-minded determination to succeed and make his mark in the world. He realised that some people viewed him as a monomaniac but he was convinced that, with his theory of the unconscious mind, he had touched upon one of the great secrets of nature. His granddaughter, Sophie Freud, claimed that he had always thought he would become a great man. Few would dispute that he achieved this. Whether he exaggerated evidence or not, one has to admire his will and determination to take the most complex structure in the universe – the human mind – and seek to explore it. Fraud or not, Freud provided much food for thought.

Perhaps it suits modern-day critics of psychoanalysis to overemphasise Freud's contemporary influence. The great mathematician A.N. Whitehead[8] once claimed that 'a science that hesitates to forget its founders is lost', so perhaps it's time to move on from Freud. Contemporary psychoanalysis can still be seen to have at the very least three points in its favour. First, it emphasises the importance of child development in relation to later adult personality; second, it emphasises the importance of human relationships to psychological well-being; third, it provides a language for exploring and expressing all kinds of feelings.[9] For example, the Little Hans case study was the first time that Freud used the term 'transference' in his writings. Transference is the displacement of one's unresolved anxieties and conflicts on to a substitute object. Hans's anxieties towards his father were transferred on to a substitute object – in his case, horses. The phobic object became a useful vehicle for the expression of his feelings.

Herbert Graf: the adult 'Hans'

So what became of Little Hans? Some critics argued that Freud's intervention in Hans's life had robbed the boy of his innocence and foretold of an evil future for the poor child. Hans was even portrayed as a victim of psychoanalysis. Freud predicted this response in his original paper when he wrote, 'I must enquire what harm was done to Hans by dragging to light in him complexes such as are not only repressed by children but dreaded by their parents?' Freud suggested that doctors who misunderstood the nature of psychoanalysis would mistakenly think that wicked instincts were strengthened by being made conscious. He argued that the result of the analysis was that Hans recovered; he ceased to be afraid of horses and developed an even more friendly relationship with his father. Indeed he reports Hans as saying to his father, 'I thought you knew everything, as you knew about that horse.'

Freud lost contact with Hans in 1911 but there was to be one last meeting between the two of them. In the spring of 1922, Herbert Graf, now aged 19, strolled into Freud's consulting rooms. Freud reports a strapping youth who was perfectly well with no apparent troubles or inhibitions. He was emotionally stable despite experiencing his parents' divorce. Herbert had continued to live with his father (perhaps supporting Freud's view of Herbert's close relationship with his father) whereas his sister, of whom he was extremely fond, had gone to live with their mother. Herbert reported that when he had read the case history of Little Hans he did not realise it had been written about him!

Herbert Graf, like his father, made a career in the musical arts. After working on various operas in Germany, Switzerland and Austria, Herbert moved to the United States in 1936 when he was 33 years old. Here his career took off and he secured the prestigious position of director of the Metropolitan Opera in New York. Following a successful period there, he moved back to his European roots, directed Maria Callas in Florence and was involved in acclaimed opera productions at Covent Garden and in Salzburg. He was director of the Zurich Opera from 1960 to 1962 and also became director of the Opera of Geneva. Herbert Graf was also a published author. In his 1951 book *Opera for the People*, he wrote at length about all aspects of opera production. He was described as a great man of the theatre, brilliantly creative and particularly welcoming to young artists.

Herbert entitled a four-part interview he gave to *Opera News*[10] 'Memoirs of an invisible man' – the title a reference to his role as one who was always working behind the scenes, never on stage. The choice of a musical career shows a clear identification with his father, but it has been suggested that directing from behind the scenes was also an identification with Freud's invisible role in his analysis.[11]

Colleagues and acquaintances described Herbert as a man of great charm and intelligence. However, he was also portrayed with a few character flaws. It is reported that certain undesirable aspects of his personality were evident to all who worked with him, even if these had remained unnoticed by Freud all those years earlier. He was also described as a lover of both fine wines and pretty women. Herbert did not seem to have been particularly successful in love and did not have a family. Some have even suggested that such facts might be taken as (surely rather weak) evidence that his childhood analysis had not been as successful as Freud claimed. Alternatively, one could argue that Herbert's career was as successful as it was in spite of the psychotherapy, rather than because of it.

Herbert Graf became ill with cancer and died in Geneva in 1973. Despite his many noteworthy accomplishments in adult life, he will perhaps forever remain most famous as Sigmund Freud's 'Little Hans'.

1. Freud, S. (1909) Two case histories: Little Hans and the 'Rat Man'. *The Standard Edition of the Complete Psychological Works of Sigmund Freud.* Volume X. London: Vintage/The Hogarth Press (reprinted, 2000).

2. Freud, S. (1905) *Three Essays on the Theory of Sexuality.* Pelican Freud Library, Vol. 7. Harmondsworth: Penguin.

3. It was subsequently found that the horse was merely responding to visual cues from its master and did not have any special mathematical abilities.

4. Graf, M. (1942) Reminiscences of Professor Sigmund Freud. *Psychoanalytic Quarterly* 11, pp. 465–76.

5. Gross, R. (2003) *Key Studies in Psychology* (4th edn). London: Hodder & Stoughton, Chapter 19.

6. Tallis, R. (1996) Burying Freud. *Lancet* 347, pp. 669–71.

7. Masson, J. (1985) *The Assault on Truth: Freud's Suppression of the Seduction Theory.* London: Penguin.

8. Whitehead, A.N. (1929) *The Aims of Education and Other Essays.* New York: Macmillan/Free Press, p. 162.

9. For an excellent extended essay on this topic, see Jeremy Holmes's 'The assault on Freud' at http://human-nature.com/freud/holmes.html.

10. Graf, H. (1972) Memoirs of an invisible man: a dialogue with Francis Rizzo. *Opera News*: 5 February, pp. 25–8; 12 February, pp. 26–9; 19 February, pp. 26–9; 26 February, pp. 26–9.

11. Holland, N. (1986) Not so little Hans: identity and ageing, in K. Woodward and M. Schwartz (eds) *Memory and Desire.* Bloomington, Ind.: Indiana University Press.

The three faces of Eve: the story of Chris Sizemore

Multiple personality disorder (MPD), also called Dissociative Identity Disorder,[1] was almost unknown until two American psychiatrists (Corbett Thigpen and Hervey Cleckley) published their case study in the 1950s. They described a patient they were treating who possessed three distinct personalities they called Eve White, Eve Black and Jane. Each personality was separate and behaved in an entirely different way to the others. The subsequent award-winning film The Three Faces of Eve, *which was based on the case, brought MPD to much wider public attention. Along with further cases that have caught the public imagination – depicted most notably in the 1970s book and film* Sybil *– this resulted in MPD changing from being a largely unknown and seemingly rare condition to a widely recognised and much more commonly diagnosed disorder. In recent years, however, academics have started to question whether MPD actually exists as a 'real' disorder or whether it is an 'iatrogenic' disorder – the creation of therapists, 'placed' in the minds of their suggestible and vulnerable patients.*

What is MPD?

Multiple Personality Disorder (MPD) is one of the dissociative[2] psychiatric disorders, its most noticeable symptom being that the person has at least one alternative, or 'alter', personality that controls behaviour. The 'alters' occur spontaneously and involuntarily, and in the main function completely independently of one another. In 1994, the American Psychiatric Association's DSM-IV (*Diagnostic Statistical Manual*) replaced the designation of MPD with DID: dissociative identity disorder. Although the diagnostic title has changed in the USA, the old label (MPD) is still used in the UK and is favoured in this chapter since it remains the better-known and, arguably, more descriptive label.

The change of name in the USA has not altered the list of symptoms, which are diverse and vary from patient to patient, so it is difficult to describe a 'typical' case of MPD. Someone suffering from MPD can have any number of 'alter' personalities, typically up to 20 or 30. There is usually one 'core' personality that copes with ordinary everyday life. This personality is usually unaware of the presence of the other personalities or, if it is aware, this is in only an indirect way (for example, evidence that it must have done something when it has no memory of doing it). Each 'alter' personality may know about all the others and may sometimes even form friendships or alliances with one or more to work against the others! Many of these 'alter' personalities are not fully developed and remain fragmentary. They can be of different ages, either sex and even any nationality. Every personality has a separate identity from the others (which might involve different gestures, handwriting, speech and body image). A person with MPD could have hallucinations so marked that they actually perceive a different personality in the mirror.[3]

History of MPD

Although certainly not well known prior to the Thigpen and Cleckley case study of Eve, MPD has a relatively long history. As long ago as 1784, a country estate worker called Victor Race living in Soissons, France, was said to have symptoms similar to those of MPD. One day, Victor fell into an altered state of consciousness where his usual slowness of thought was replaced by a bright and quick-witted personality. When he recovered his usual state of consciousness he had no recollection of these events or the transformation that had taken place in his personality.[4]

Perhaps the first detailed account of MPD was published by Eberhard Gmelin in 1791 and involved a 21-year-old woman from Stuttgart who suddenly took on the personality and language of a French woman. In her altered state she believed that she had fled to Germany to escape the French Revolution. In this state of awareness, she could speak only rudimentary German with a French accent. The woman was unaware of the existence of this altered state.

Although there were subsequent reports in the literature on multiple personalities, most notably Morton Prince's Miss Beauchamp study[5] (a study cited by Thigpen and Cleckley), its infrequent occurrence led to MPD being largely ignored in psychiatric circles. Indeed, Thigpen and Cleckley wrote that, 'multiple personality is a rarity in psychopathology'. They were to change all that with their case study of Eve, published in 1954.[6]

Eve

Corbett Thigpen was a psychiatrist who had been treating a 25-year-old married woman for 'severe and blinding headaches'. She also reported having 'blackouts' following the headaches. Thigpen and his colleague Hervey Cleckley called her 'Eve White' in their subsequent writings. After a series of infrequent therapeutic sessions they concluded that her symptoms were caused by a typical mixture of marital conflicts and personal frustrations. She had once forgotten the details of a previous therapy session, but had later recalled it under hypnosis. Nothing about her case stood out. One day, however, out of the blue, Thigpen received a puzzling, unsigned letter that he realised must have been written by Eve White. He noted, though, that the last paragraph had obviously been written by someone else. The immature content and handwriting style suggested it was the work of a child.

Questioned about the letter on her next visit, Eve denied any knowledge of it. She recalled starting the letter but believed she had destroyed it unfinished. She became quite agitated during the interview and suddenly asked whether hearing an imaginary voice was a sign of insanity. Thigpen was intrigued. Eve had never previously displayed or mentioned any such symptoms. Before Thigpen had a chance to answer Eve's question, she put both hands to her head as if overcome by a shooting pain. After a brief moment, she dropped her hands, gave a quick and reckless smile and in a bright voice said 'Hi there, Doc!' The familiar retiring, conventional Eve White had been replaced by a newcomer with a devilish and carefree personality who talked at length about Eve White as a different person. On being asked who she was, she replied 'Oh, I'm Eve Black.' To all intents and purposes, Thigpen had been joined by a completely different person.

Over the next 14 months, during a series of interviews totalling approximately 100 hours, extensive material was gathered about the behaviour and inner life of both Eve White and Eve Black. Thigpen and Cleckley reported that Eve Black had existed as an independent personality since Eve White's childhood and was a product of disruptive events in childhood. Furthermore, while Eve White was unaware of Eve Black, Eve Black was aware of Eve White: when not 'out', Eve Black was aware of what Eve White was doing, whereas the reverse was not true. Although Eve Black would often spontaneously 'pop out', it was found that, initially, she could be called forth only under hypnosis. After further therapeutic sessions, hypnosis was no longer necessary and Cleckley could simply call forth whichever of the personalities he wished to talk to. One unfortunate side-effect of this was that Eve Black found herself more able to 'take over' Eve White than had previously been the case.

Thigpen and Cleckley suggested that the fragmentation of Eve's personality had been a way of coping with experiences she could not bear. This suggestion seemed to be supported by Chris Sizemore's[7] biography (Christine Sizemore is Eve's real name), where she outlined a number of traumatic incidents she had experienced while growing up in North Carolina during the Depression.[8] The first involved her witnessing the dead body of a man being retrieved from a waterlogged ditch. It was surmised that he had fallen in and drowned when drunk the night before. Chris reports that she 'saw' on the bridge, looking down on the scene, a little girl whose red hair shone brightly in the morning sun and whose eyes were bright blue, calm and unafraid. Another incident of note involved her mother, who was holding a glass milk bottle when it broke. Realising that her daughter was directly beneath the broken bottle, Chris's mother, Zueline, hugged the broken shards to her body in order to protect her. In doing this one of the shards of glass cut into her mother's left wrist. The sight of blood terrified Chris who, despite being told to fetch help, ran away and collapsed in a heap in the corner of the room. The red-haired girl with the cold blue eyes appeared once again and stood watching the red blood mix with the white milk for some time before running to get help.

Another traumatic incident was to follow shortly. Chris's father used to work at the local sawmill. A whistle would sound to mark the start and finish of the day's work. One day, the whistle sounded at 10.25 am to indicate that there had been an accident at the mill. All the relatives of the workers immediately hurried to the mill to see what had happened. Chris was among them and arrived to see the grotesque sight of a man's body sliced in half above the waist. Each half lay either side of the saw, a short distance apart. Chris noticed that one of his arms had been severed. Here was a body physically separated into three distinct parts.

Chris later wrote that a child should never have seen such horrible things and that she could not bear the sight of them. She suggested that perhaps the red-haired girl was someone who could watch what she herself could not face.

Despite such incidents Chris lived in fairly favourable circumstances compared to many children brought up in Depression-era America. For most of her childhood, she lived with her large extended family on their productive farm. The family had been fortunate to invest in land at just the right time, and working the land meant that they avoided many of the dreadful hardships of the time. Nevertheless, Chris was always finding herself in trouble. She would do things she had been told not to and then deny having done them in the first place. These incidents, and the subsequent 'lying', exasperated her parents and led to increasingly severe punishments; as was common at that time, these tended to be physical in nature. During such spankings, Christine often used to sob that '*She* did it!' and would continue to protest her own innocence.

One particular feature of many subsequent MPD cases is the existence of child sexual abuse. Despite numerous therapy sessions, often involving hypnosis, there was never any evidence that Eve had suffered any form of this. The catalyst for Eve's creation of 'alter' personalities seemed linked to traumatic incidents (not of a sexual nature) in her childhood.

Thigpen and Cleckley used contrasting techniques to explore Eve's personalities. Allied to the therapeutic sessions they interviewed Eve's family (her parents and husband). More often than not, the family substantiated various incidents reported by Eve Black. However, since Eve White had no access to Eve Black and Eve Black was shown to 'lie glibly and without compunction', the therapists were unable to verify all her stories. Eve White's husband and parents had noticed many of the personality changes that the therapists had witnessed but, unaware of the existence of MPD, had thought they were 'fits of temper' or her 'strange little habits' as her mother innocently called them. They had noted that her personality changes were in marked contrast to her more usual, gentle and considerate nature.

When confronted with her delinquency, Eve Black expressed amusement at 'popping out' to make mischief or enjoy some forbidden adventure only to disappear and leave Eve White to face the ensuing punishment. Eve White reported bewilderment at being punished for misdemeanours of which she had no memory. Eve Black followed a hedonistic lifestyle that involved, among other things, buying expensive and unnecessary clothing and flirting with strangers in cheap nightclubs. She enjoyed going out and getting drunk, aware that it would be Eve White who would wake up with the hangover, unaware of the causes of it or what had happened the night before. As far as her clothes purchases were concerned, when confronted with them Eve White denied all knowledge of them. Horrified to the same degree as her husband by the thought of being plunged into debt she promptly took them all back to the shop for a refund. Unable to explain how the clothes had got into her wardrobe, she suspected her husband of planting them there to make it appear that she was going 'insane'.

Eve White had a four-year-old daughter who, because of Eve's psychiatric problems, was living with her grandparents. Having to work in a city 100 miles from the girl had caused Eve White a great deal of further unhappiness and despair. Eve Black was aware of the child but had no feelings towards her. She generally ignored the child or treated her with complete indifference. On one occasion, however, when the 'little brat got on my nerves', she admitted trying to strangle her before Eve White's husband intervened. Aware of this incident, but unaware of her part in it, Eve White voluntarily committed herself to a psychiatric unit for some time afterwards. Eve Black totally denied marriage to Eve White's husband, whom she despised. Thigpen and Cleckley believed that the Whites' marriage would probably have foundered eventually, given their incompatibility, but the presence of Eve Black ensured that they separated. Eve Black did not purposely set out to harm Eve White through maliciousness or cruelty, but felt no guilt or compassion if harm happened.

Psychological testing

Thigpen and Cleckley also conducted electroencephalogram (EEG) tests and a number of psychometric and projective tests, including intelligence tests, memory tests and Rorschach (ink blot) tests, on both Eve White and Eve Black. A summary of their findings is shown in Table 16.1.

These psychological tests were conducted by an independent clinical psychologist called Dr Leopold Winter. His report supported the diagnosis of MPD and gave further details of the contrast in the personalities of the 'two' women. He argued that the projective tests showed that Eve Black's personality was the result of a regression to a time before the marriage. He argued that there were not two different personalities but one personality at different times of her life. Adopting a psychoanalytic approach, Winter suggested that Eve White experienced great anxiety over her role as a wife and mother. Only with a supreme amount of effort could she function in either or both of these roles. The effort required caused her further anxiety and an ever increasing hostility to her dual roles. This hostility was unacceptable to her and so she employed a defence mechanism – in this case regression – to cope with these feelings of anxiety: she removed the conflicting situation from her conscious awareness. At the same time, she (unconsciously) played the role of Eve Black in order to direct her hostility towards Eve White, for whom she showed utter contempt because of her lack of foresight overall and for her lack of courage in trying to solve the situation. (The 'defence mechanism' explanation echoes the explanation of Little Hans's phobia, see Chapter 15.)

During their exploration of the case, Thigpen and Cleckley came across a distant relative who revealed that Eve White had been married before. Eve White denied any such union, and so did Eve Black. However, after further repeated questioning, Eve Black did admit she had been married previously, but that she had been the bride, not Eve White! Eve Black reported that one night when Eve White was working many miles from her parents' home she had 'popped out' and gone drinking and dancing. After a particularly wild night she had, half jokingly, agreed to marry a man she scarcely knew. Although no official records of the marriage could be located, Eve Black reported that there was certainly some sort of informal marriage ceremony and she believed that she had married him.

She lived with this man as his 'wife' for a number of months. During this time, Eve Black seemed to be dominant over Eve White. Eve White had no recollection of any such marriage. Eve Black claimed that this was because she was able to erase certain aspects of Eve White's memory.

Table 16.1 Summary of findings from diagnostic tests conducted on Eve White and Eve Black

Characteristic	Eve White	Eve Black
Personality	Demure, almost saintly	Egocentric, party girl
Face	Quiet sweetness, contained sadness	Eyes dance with mischief, expression of wilfulness, will never know sadness
Clothes	Simple, neat, conservative	A little provocative
Posture	Slight stoop; dignified careful movements	A touch of sexiness pervades every gesture
Voice	Soft, feminine restraint	Coarse, teasing, witty constant use of vernacular
Character/attitude	Steadfast, industrious, contemplative, passive strength, lacks initiative; seldom animated, rarely jokes	Whim-like, momentary, spontaneous, unthinking, callous, prankster, ready wit, amusing and immediately likeable
Intelligence (IQ) test score	110 (score may have been affected by anxiety)	104 (score may have been affected by indifference)
Memory test performance	Superior to Eve Black and above that expected in comparison to IQ score; a surprising finding given her history of amnesia	Inferior to Eve White but consistent with intelligence score
Rorschach (ink blot) test results	Very anxious about her role as wife and mother; has obsessive compulsive traits	Slight hysterical tendency but healthier than Eve White
Other projective test results	Repression	Regression
Physical health	No allergies present	Allergy to nylon

Treatment of Eve

After about eight months of psychiatric treatment Eve White seemed to be making encouraging progress. She had not been troubled by her headaches or 'blackouts'. She had been promoted at her work (as a telephone operator) and had made some new friends. Eve Black was bored at Eve White's work and seldom appeared during working hours. She continued to 'pop out' infrequently during leisure hours in order to pick up unsuitable men.

At this point, Eve White's headaches and blackouts returned. It had been noticed that these 'blackouts' often occurred when the two personalities were changing, but Eve Black denied all knowledge of them. Eve Black appeared curious as to the cause of the blackouts and was quoted as saying, intriguingly, 'I don't know where we go, but go we do.' On more than one occasion, Eve White was found by a housemate lying on the floor unconscious. There appeared to be no doubt that Eve's condition was deteriorating. She was threatened with detention in a psychiatric institution in the hope that Eve Black would start to co-operate with the therapy for fear of being similarly confined. One day, during a session where she was recounting an incident from her childhood, she closed her eyes and fell silent. About two minutes later she opened her eyes and looked around the room in a state of bewilderment before turning to Thigpen and asking in an unknown husky voice, 'Who are you?' A third personality had emerged, one who called herself Jane.

It was immediately obvious that Jane did not possess Eve Black's faults, was more mature, vivid and capable, and possessed more initiative than Eve White. Jane was also aware of what both Eve White and Eve Black did. She was a mechanism through which the therapists could tell whether Eve Black was lying. Although Jane did not feel responsible for Eve White's role of wife and mother, she showed a great deal of compassion for Eve White's predicament. Jane started to take over some of Eve White's tasks, both at home and at work. Jane showed a ready willingness to take an active role in the upbringing of Eve White's child.

Soon after Jane appeared the three personalities were given EEG tests. It was possible to make a clear distinction between the readings of Eve Black and the other two personalities. Eve Black's relaxation rhythm was recorded at 12.5 cycles per second, which showed her to be the most tense of the three personalities and on the borderline of abnormal. Eve White was next, with Jane the least tense – both the latter's recordings were in the normal range.

Since MPD is the dissociation of one personality, earlier on in the therapy Thigpen and Cleckley had attempted to reintegrate the original two personalities. They had tried to do this by calling out for both personalities at once. This had resulted for Eve in a violent headache and emotional stress so severe that Thigpen and Cleckley concluded it would have been unwise to proceed in this way. However, with the more confident Jane now emerging, the possibility existed of getting her to integrate all the personalities and remain in full control.

Thigpen and Cleckley wrestled with the idea of trying to promote the personality of Jane at the expense of the other two personalities. However, they wrote that Jane shared their reluctance to participate in any act that would contribute to Eve White's extinction. Although the mother of Eve White's child would still *physically* exist, Jane did not feel she was the actual mother. Eve White herself recognised the possibility of Jane taking over and seemed to accept that her own extinction might enable Jane to succeed in the maternal role in which she had failed. In effect, Eve White seemed willing to 'lay down her life' for the benefit of her child.

Near the end of the case study, Jane wrote a letter to Thigpen recounting an incident whereby Eve White risked her life by jumping into the road to grab a small child from being hit by a car. She wrote that Eve White walked away hugging the relieved little boy. She tells how she (Jane) had to emerge and return the boy to a nearby policeman for fear of Eve White being arrested for kidnapping! Jane wrote that she couldn't face such a worthy person dying. Jane argued that Eve White should survive, not her. Furthermore she wrote that she could no longer feel Eve Black and wondered whether she had simply given up. This last event hinted that the personalities were becoming successfully resolved.

Questions to consider

This was not to be the end of the case, however. Thigpen and Cleckley wrote up the Eve case study into a book[9] and this spawned a subsequent film[10] of the same name (*The Three Faces of Eve*, starring Joanne Woodward). Both the book and the film were huge hits. The book was translated into 22 different languages and received a number of literary non-fiction awards, and Joanne Woodward won both a Golden Globe and an Oscar (Best Actress) for her portrayal of Eve in the film. Both the book and film also helped bring MPD to public prominence.

Some people questioned Thigpen and Cleckley's original reporting of the case, and issues such as the question of whether Eve was a 'hoax' were raised. Thigpen and Cleckley, however, had spent a great deal of time with Eve and believed that not even a professional actor could have taken on the different roles she portrayed so convincingly and consistently. Thigpen and Cleckley made efforts to substantiate all information reported and were able to corroborate much of it through relatives. They also asked Dr Winter, as an independent expert, to conduct various physiological and psychological tests, and these appeared to confirm the existence of distinct personalities.

However, as with any case study, it is difficult to know whether the findings can be generalised beyond the specific case in question. Was Eve a unique case or was she typical of other MPD cases? The emergence of different identities and the amnesic aspects of them are consistent with 'typical' MPD (if such a thing exists), but the lack of evidence of any child abuse is unusual.[11] This case study relied on retrospective-memory accounts of events and these may not have been particularly reliable. The events related by Eve Black, a consummate liar, are particularly open to this criticism. With over 100 hours of therapy over a 14-month period there is no doubt that the therapists forged a close relationship with Eve. Although this may be seen as an important part of the therapy, there is a danger that the therapists selectively reported the data in a biased way.

There were a number of ethical issues to consider in this case study. Thigpen and Cleckley recognised this when it came to the possible 'killing' of one of the personalities, and they concluded that 'we have not judged ourselves as wise enough to make active decisions or exert personal influence in shaping what impends'. Some have argued that, by publishing the study, Thigpen and Cleckley intruded into Eve's life in an unnecessary way and, given her problems, it remains unclear whether they got her *informed* consent prior to publication. In essence, their good fortune (increased status and financial gain) came about as a direct result of exploiting Eve's misfortune. However, they did not reveal Eve's real identity and they argued that they helped to raise the profile of an important psychiatric disorder, which may have helped other people suffering from MPD.

Eve's reappearance

Nothing much more was heard of the case until 1977 when Chris Sizemore revealed herself to be the real Eve (in the book *I'm Eve*, published that year). Some of the details of the case she disclosed were different to those reported by Thigpen and Cleckley. She revealed that she had approximately 22 personalities and that these were present both before and after the therapy. She further asserted that she had not been cured by Thigpen and Cleckley. She had actually continued her therapy with another doctor called Tony Tsitos. In a more recent book[12] she stated that she was finally cured after having had MPD for 45 years and after undergoing 20 years of therapy.

Sizemore has gone from strength to strength and has given much of her time to promoting understanding of MPD. She has looked into the role of art as part of the therapeutic process, given numerous talks about MPD for the American Mental Health Association and received a host of awards for her efforts.

The Sybil phenomenon?

Following on from the case study of Eve, the best-known MPD case study surrounds the case of 'Sybil', a patient who developed as many as 16 separate personalities in order to deal with horrendous physical and sexual child abuse. In 1973, the case was subsequently dramatised into a best-selling book[13] by the journalist Flora Rheta Schreiber. The book became one of the best-selling nonfiction books of the year. As with *The Three Faces of Eve*, the book was quickly made into a successful television film called *Sybil*[14], again featuring Joanne Woodward (who had played Eve in the earlier film), this time in the role of therapist Dr Cornelia Wilbur. Again, in an echo of the earlier film, Sally Field won an Emmy for her portrayal of Sybil.

However, in contrast to the study of Eve there are serious question marks over the veracity of the Sybil case. Herbert Spiegel, a respected psychiatrist, knew both Wilbur and Sybil. In fact, he is briefly mentioned in the Acknowledgements section of *Sybil*, but nowhere else in the book. This is a surprising omission given that he treated Sybil on occasion, and she even participated in some of his hypnosis demonstrations at Columbia's University College. Spiegel categorised Sybil as highly suggestible, indicating that Wilbur may have induced the personalities later reported. Sybil's may have been a classic example of an iatrogenic illness. This is one where the illness is induced in the patient by a physician's activity, manner or therapy. In essence, in Sybil's case the personalities may have been a by-product of Wilbur's suggestions during hypnosis. There are also other damaging claims about the processes involved in reporting the study. For example, Wilbur promoted the idea of the book when she found she could not get her study printed in reputable journals. There are also claims that Schreiber, the book's author, insisted that Sybil be 'cured' before she would agree to write the book.

Despite such criticisms the combined influence of the cases of Eve and Sybil led to increased recognition of MPD among both health professionals and public alike.

What happened to Thigpen and Cleckley?

Cleckley and Thigpen were already respected academics prior to the publication of the Eve case study, and continued with their careers. Their book in particular led to international recognition. In a subsequent follow-up paper[15] on the incidence of MPD, published 25 years after the Eve case study, Thigpen and Cleckley warned against the over-reporting of MPD. Due to their expertise, they had had hundreds of patients specifically referred to them by their therapists, who believed they were suffering from MPD. However, Thigpen and Cleckley argued that, in over 30 years of combined practice in which they had seen thousands of patients, there was only one other case that they believed was a genuine example of MPD. They described the procession of these patients to their practice in Georgia as some sort of 'pilgrimage'. They even reported one woman introducing all her different 'personalities' over the phone to them using a different voice for each one!

Thigpen and Cleckley discussed their concern that some patients, and indeed some therapists, seek to draw attention to themselves by a diagnosis of MPD. They cited patients who moved from one therapist to another until they found one who would confirm their own diagnosis of MPD. Although recognising the need for help in such patients Thigpen and Cleckley did not recognise the high incidence of reported MPD. They even suggested that there is unhealthy competition among some patients and therapists to see who can reveal the most personalities. They suggested that the main reasons behind such behaviour are the attention bestowed once diagnosis is made and the secondary gain these patients obtain, namely the avoidance of responsibility for their actions. Thigpen and Cleckley stated that this secondary gain is most noticeable in criminal cases where a patient can gain a great deal by a diagnosis of MPD. They cited the celebrated case of Billy Milligan,[16] who was initially diagnosed as having MPD (a diagnosis also made by Dr Cornelia Wilbur of 'Sybil' fame). After treatment, he was judged competent for trial and then suffered a relapse prior to the hearing. Thigpen and Cleckley suggested that a desire to avoid responsibility for one's actions in such cases might motivate a person to dissociate further. Of course, Milligan claimed to be a genuine case of MPD, but perhaps surprisingly (or cleverly?) agreed with Thigpen and Cleckley's general argument that many cases of MPD are 'created' by the psychiatrists themselves.

Thigpen and Cleckley also questioned whether a diagnosis of MPD should actually relieve a person of complete responsibility for their actions. They argued that although the main personality may have no memory of the behaviour of their 'alter' personalities, the 'alter' personalities are aware of their behavioural actions and, as such, never perform actions that might threaten the survival of the total person. They concluded that the diagnosis of MPD should be reserved for those very few people, such as Chris Sizemore, who are fragmented in the most extreme manner.

Cleckley, a Rhodes scholar who attended Oxford University in 1926, was already a professor of psychiatry and neurology at the University of Georgia Medical School prior to the 1957 publication of *The Three Faces of Eve*. He died on 28 January 1984, aged 79.

Following a similar career pattern, Hervey Thigpen practised medicine for over 50 years and had become a clinical professor of psychiatry at the Georgia Medical School by the time of his retirement in 1987. Thigpen died on 19 March 1999, aged 80.

MPD: real or created?

To this day, the diagnosis of MPD remains very unreliable. Some of the symptoms of MPD, such as auditory hallucinations, the creation of fantasy worlds and self-mutilation, can also occur with schizophrenia. Because of this there is often a confusion between MPD and schizophrenia. MPD is not a form of schizophrenia. In contrast to MPD, schizophrenia is a type of psychosis where contact with reality and insight are impaired. In essence, schizophrenia involves a 'splitting of one mind', whereas MPD involves the construction of many whole personalities. Schizophrenic patients can usually report their hallucinations and delusions to a therapist, whereas a patient with MPD cannot do so due to profound amnesia. A biological or chemical cause of schizophrenia has been found, whereas a biological cause for MPD has yet to be determined. Perhaps reflecting differences in diagnostic practices, MPD is far more prevalent in some western countries (for example, the USA and the Netherlands) than others (for example, the UK and Germany). In the first half of the twentieth century there were a handful of cases reported in the literature. With its introduction in the psychiatric diagnosis manual in 1980, MPD cases suddenly sprang up everywhere. In a large-scale survey of the population in the city of Winnipeg, 1 per cent of the adult population was deemed to have MPD related to childhood abuse.[17]

MPD also remains primarily a western 'invention' and is rarely reported in other cultures. Do these facts and figures indicate a greater recognition and understanding of the disorder or do they suggest an iatrogenic cause to the disorder? Eighty-five per cent of MPD cases involve women. Is this because there is an established history of MPD in women, and hence the tradition is more likely to be followed by patients and therapists alike, or does it reflect the way women are treated in our society? Does it reflect a sex or gender link, or are women more likely to be the victims of child abuse and have a greater need to fragment their personality to protect themselves from such an ordeal?

Another problem involves childhood amnesia. It is estimated that in 90 per cent of cases of MPD the precipitating cause is childhood trauma (most commonly that involving sexual abuse). However, children generally remember virtually nothing of their childhood prior to the age of three and very little accurately before the age of five. Proponents of MPD argue that the 'alter' personality holds on to the painful childhood memories because these can't be faced by the victim. Richard Kluft[18] could corroborate only 15 per cent of reported accounts of childhood abuse in MPD patients. This low figure does not, in itself, prove they didn't occur. After all, it is in the abuser's interests to hide, destroy and deny all such evidence. Elizabeth Loftus,[19] one of the world's leading experts in memory research, discounts the idea that young children can recall particularly painful memories. Intriguingly, she poses the question that if this is so, why do children not recall having injections or being circumcised? A possible answer from a psychoanalyst might be because they repress such memories.

In terms of the diagnosis of MPD today, there is an additional problem. Ironically, this could be said to have its origins in the case study of Eve. Thigpen and Cleckley's case study became so well known and spawned such a fascination in the public with MPD that today 'no case has been found in which MPD, as now conceived, is proven to have emerged through unconscious processes without any shaping or preparation by external factors such as physicians or the media'.[20] In the case of Sybil, she even obligingly read *The Three Faces of Eve* and was fascinated by it. It was argued that she had been excessively influenced by mass-media coverage of the disorder. In essence, she had been taught how to act the part.

In a series of well-known studies in the mid-1980s, Nicholas Spanos[21] found he could convince people that they possessed 'alter' personalities with very little suggestion on his part. In many cases, he did this even without the need to hypnotise them. He further argued that repressed memories of childhood abuse and multiple personality disorder are 'rule-governed social constructions established, legitimated, and maintained through social interaction'. He said, in other words, that the majority of MPD cases are created by therapists with the co-operation of their patients and the rest of society. As can be seen, there is a chasm of opinion in psychiatric circles about the authenticity and diagnosis of MPD. Whether MPD is a real or iatrogenic disorder, patients who believe they have the condition should, on the whole, deserve help, not blame.

In 1987, Paul Chodoff[22] wrote that 'there is a tendency in the history of psychiatry for certain conditions to be recognised, rise in popularity and then decline in accordance with largely cultural determinants'. Is this the fate that awaits MPD?

1. There remains considerable dispute about the most appropriate term to use. See the article entitled 'Dual personality, multiple personality, dissociative identity disorder – what's in a name?' at http://www.dissociation.com/index/Definition/ for further details.

2. Dissociation is a mechanism that allows the mind to separate or compartmentalise certain memories or thoughts from normal consciousness. The distinctive feature of dissociation is 'a disruption in the usually integrated functions of consciousness, memory, identity, or perception of the environment' (source: *Diagnostic Statistical Manual*, 1994).

3. Sileo, C.C. (1993) Multiple personalities: the experts are split. *Insight on the News* 9(43), October, pp. 18ff.

4. Crabtree, A. (1993) *From Mesmer to Freud: Magnetic Sleep and the Roots of Psychological Healing.* New Haven: Yale University Press.

5. Prince, M. (1906) *The Dissociation of Personality.* New York: Longman/Green.

6. Thigpen, C.H. and Cleckley, H.M. (1954) A case of multiple personality. *Journal of Abnormal and Social Psychology* 49, pp. 135–51.

7. Sizemore, C.C. and Pittillo, E.S. (1977) *I'm Eve.* New York: Doubleday & Co.

8. In a subsequent book (*A Mind of My Own*, published in 1989), Sizemore argued that her personalities had been present at birth.

9. Thigpen, C.H. and Cleckley, H.M. (1957) *The Three Faces of Eve.* USA: Secker & Warburg.

10. *The Three Faces of Eve* (1957), directed by Nunnally Johnson. Twentieth Century Fox.

11. The existence of child abuse is a fairly consistent feature of *subsequent* cases of MPD, but was not the case in 1954.

12. Sizemore, C.C. (1989) *A Mind of My Own.* New York: William Morrow.

13. Schreiber, F.R. (1973) *Sybil. The True Story of a Woman Possessed by Sixteen Separate Personalities.* USA: Penguin.

14. *Sybil* (1976), directed by Daniel Petrie. CBS Fox.

15. Thigpen, C.H. and Cleckley, H.M. (1984) On the incidence of multiple personality disorder: a brief communication. *International Journal of Clinical and Experimental Hypnosis* 32(2), pp. 63–6.

16. Keyes, D. (1995 reprint) *The Minds of Billy Milligan.* USA: Bantam Books.

17. Ross, C.A. (1991) Epidemiology of multiple personality disorder and dissociation. *Journal of the Psychiatric Clinics of North America* 14(3), September, pp. 503–17.

18. Kluft, R.P. (1985) *Childhood Antecedents of Multiple Personality Disorder* (Clinical Insights Monograph). Washington: American Psychological Association.

19. Loftus, E.F (1997) *The Myth of Repressed Memories.* New York, NY: St Martins Press.

20. Merskey, H. (1992) The manufacture of personalities – the production of multiple personality disorder. *British Journal of Psychiatry* 160, pp. 327–40

21. Spanos, N.P. (1996) *Multiple Identities and False Memories: A Sociocognitive Perspective.* Washington: American Psychological Association.

22. Chodoff, P. (1987) Effects of the new economic climate on psychotherapeutic practice. *American Journal of Psychiatry* 144, pp. 1293–7.